BREASTFEEDING THE

ADOPTED BABY

Breastfeeding the

Adopted Baby

by

DEBRA STEWART PETERSON

Foreword by
BARBARA HEISER, RN, BSN, IBCLC

Edited by
JUDY MINAMI, MSC, CLE

CORONA PUBLISHING COMPANY
San Antonio, Texas
1994

For information, contact:

CORONA PUBLISHING CO.
P.O. Drawer 12407
San Antonio, Texas 78212

ISBN 0-931722-43-8
Manufactured in the United States of America

This book is dedicated to my husband, David, and all my friends in La Leche League, with a special mention to Judy Nelson and Linda Munhall for the love, help, and support they freely gave as I chose to breastfeed my adopted babies. Special thanks to Debra Kurtz at Medela, Barbara Heiser, and Judy Minami for all their support. I would also like to thank Susan Stewart Washburn and her daughter Michelle, as well as Daralyn Star and her son Joseph, for modeling in our photographs. Photography was done by Weber State University, Pinnacle Marketing, and Medela, Inc.

TABLE OF CONTENTS

LIST OF ILLUSTRATIONS

PREFACE

I carefully wrote this as a handbook for mothers who desire to breastfeed their adopted babies. Many myths exist, and many medical-professional and lay-people do not understand the simplicity involved in breastfeeding an adopted baby. This book is written to be easily understood by the reader, not as a resource book to the medical-professional.

My goal is to assist any mother whose choice is to breastfeed her adopted baby; to empower her to breastfeed and to help her develop the confidence and support she will need.

I have tried to answer all the questions I had when breastfeeding my first adopted baby, as well as those questions I have been asked over the last ten years.

Much of what I have written is from my own experiences and from that of mothers and doctors with whom I have worked and associated. References to material about subjects you may want to discuss with your medical-professional are given throughout the book.

Many will try to make breastfeeding appear to be a difficult process when in fact it is a beautifully simple, natural process.

May our babies drink the milk that their mothers and God created for them.

FOREWORD
by Barbara Heiser, RN, BSN, IBCLC

Becoming a mother is an integral part of womanhood. Presently, however, we see many couples frustrated by infertility, a large number of whom reach out to adoption as an alternative way of birthing their family. Many of these mothers, in particular, feel robbed of pregnancy and as if they have somehow failed. We, as health care professionals, need to help them adjust to their new family as normally as possible without the biological and hormonal benefits of pregnancy. Breastfeeding can be one avenue to assist in bonding and nurturing within these special families.

"Current research findings, and today's *New York Times*, support the conclusion that human milk constituents are not interchangeable with those of other nutrient sources. The nutrition, immunologic, hypoallergenic, psychologic, and economic advantages of breastfeeding have been studied and are well documented in the literature . . ." (*Donna O'Hare, for the American Academy of Pediatrics testifying before the House Select Committee on Hunger, 10/3/91*).

It is important that we offer support to these new mothers to enable them to breastfeed their special babies. However, many healthcare providers do not have the knowledge or personal experience of working with an adoptive mother. In my fifteen years' experience, I have had the pleasure of working with many mothers who have made this choice and were rewarded by it.

This book is a practical guide which answers many questions the adoptive mother might ask as she makes her infant feeding choice or begins her breastfeeding experience. It provides information, helpful resources, and encouragement from one mother who has had the experience of nursing two adopted babies. Debra has written from her heart to other adoptive mothers so that they may benefit from her experience as they endeavor to make an informed feeding choice and then feel supported in that choice.

Chapter One

ADVANTAGES OF BREASTFEEDING

Why would a mother want to nurse her adopted baby? For the same advantages a birth mother gains by nursing her baby. The one advantage at the top of the list (whenever discussed in groups) is *bonding*, the attachment that occurs between a baby and its parents. Breastfeeding seems to deepen bonding due to skin-to-skin contact. A mother experiences an increased level of prolactin (a hormone that is naturally released in response to the infant's suckling) when she is nursing, and this is known to increase her mothering instinct. Therefore, she may be more sensitive to her baby's needs.

Bonding is also encouraged more with the father. A father can become more involved with touching and growing close to the baby through many activities other than feeding. Bathing together is a good way for baby and father to bond. Burping the baby, diapering, rubbing the baby's back, and doing baby massage all involve the father and encourage bonding.

Another reason you might choose to breastfeed is convenience—you can just sit down and nurse the baby without preparing bottles.

That's a real benefit. This is true even with breastfeeding an adopted baby. A baby is easy to nurse discreetly, especially if you practice in front of the mirror. You CAN nurse discreetly, practically anywhere.

Encouraging your baby's eye development is another benefit to breastfeeding. It's difficult for a baby to develop the proper eye muscles when lying on his back, the way most mothers position their babies to give them a bottle. When a baby breastfeeds, he looks up at an angle to view his mother's face. In so doing the baby develops eye coordination and strength.

Mouth and jaw muscle development is another advantage to breastfeeding. Babies suck entirely differently at the breast than they do on a bottle. When breastfeeding, the effort is to start milk flow; with the bottle, it is to control ready flow. Each pattern of sucking uses entirely different muscles, and thus babies who must alternate between the breast and bottle often experience nipple confusion. This is especially true in cases when the bottle does not have a NUK nipple or a Haberman feeder nipple. The Haberman Teat[1] is probably the best rubber nipple for encouraging

---

[1]Haberman Feeder Nipples, by Medela, can be ordered on the order form in the back of the book.

the baby to suck properly and allows the baby to go back and forth from bottle to breast with the least nipple confusion. It also works without negative pressure buildup in the bottle, allowing you to control the flow. With other nipples on the market, there is no control. The NUK nipple is available in almost all stores. To use the NUK properly, the baby's lips should flare out onto the widest part of the nipple. The baby will use the proper jaw muscles at the breast, and develop many face and jaw muscles as he rhythmically massages behind the nipple with his tongue and jaws to squirt the milk into his mouth. The baby is doing a lot more work, compared to sucking on a bottle (where baby doesn't expend as much energy or develop the jaw muscles in the same way as he would at the breast). The baby is doing a lot more participating. He's actively involved at the breast and more fully absorbed in the whole relationship.

The baby swallows properly when he's at the breast. He doesn't have the tongue-thrust swallow, where the tongue thrusts against the back of the top front teeth. This is the reason most of us wore braces when we were in high school. A breastfed baby's chances for braces are decreased because he learns to suck and swallow properly. Therefore, his teeth come in as correctly as possible, because this early learning predisposes him to swallowing the right way for the rest of his life. It's very difficult to learn how to swallow differently after you have been swallowing incorrectly for so many years. In fact, it's almost impossible. It's like trying to learn how to breathe differently. It's something that just comes to us so naturally.

All breastfeeding mothers appreciate that their breastfed babies smell so pretty, because breast milk is so suited to their baby's little digestive systems. Their diapers smell sweeter, and the odor doesn't take over the house. When a breastfed baby spits up on you, it doesn't have a sour smell. You don't feel like you have to run, change all your clothes, and shower, too. Babies also don't get constipated from breast milk. Formula can be very constipating, especially if it is iron fortified. Mothers' milk is rich in a highly concentrated iron that is completely utilized by your baby's body. Health professionals took both my breastfed adopted babies off iron-fortified formulas. Their iron count (hemoglobin) was very high and maintained such a good level that I was cautioned against supplementing them with any iron-fortified vitamin or formula. And I only had a partial milk supply. But, I am very careful to get sufficient iron in *my* diet.

Breastfed babies have that peaches-and-cream complexion and *very* soft skin. Many of our friends and neighbors would want to feel our daughter's skin; they couldn't believe how soft and silky it was. They thought it was because she was black. But all my breastfed babies had that soft silkiness to their skin, and yours will, too. That comes with breastfeeding.

Studies have shown that breast milk builds more brain cells.[2] And the benefits go on and on. The Surgeon General of the United States has challenged the mothers of our nation to breastfeed their babies. And the percentages in our nation are climbing for breastfed babies. It's become common knowledge that breast milk is the ideal, superior food for babies. The benefits reach clear into their adult lives. The intestinal flora established by breastfeeding alone keeps us healthier throughout our lives. Breastfeeding and bonding help us learn and meet our babies' needs. I believe if we meet our children's needs while they are young (rather than them having to learn to mother themselves), they will be more self-confident and independent when they are older.

---

[2]Lucas, et al., "Breastmilk and Subsequent Intelligence Quotient in Children Born Preterm," *Lancet* 339 (Feb. 1, 1992): 261-264.

I, and many other parents, have found this to be true.

You will soon realize there are advantages to you as a mother as much as benefits for your baby. Breastfeeding has been a beneficial way for me to begin my mothering experience. It made it easier to meet all of my babies' needs, making mothering easier, and it helped me realize that I need to meet my own needs, too. As women, our hormones seem to be conducive to calm, gentle mothering. It positively affects the entire family. Breastfeeding also seemed to help me keep my priorities in proper order. It encouraged me to stop and take time to bond with my babies. It's really difficult for a mother to try to keep up with the house and chores and the meals and all the children . . . to do everything she was doing before she got this full-time baby. And so sometimes I think Mother Nature meant for us to sit down, slow down, and take time with baby. *Lack of regular one-on-one time can inhibit the bonding influence!* Your baby needs physical contact. By sitting down and breastfeeding (or bottle feeding), the emotional needs are met as much as the physical, nutritional, and sucking needs. We're meeting a lot of needs when we take this time.

Another thing that mothers love about breastfeeding is that nighttime interruptions aren't as abrupt. Most often, a breastfeeding mother keeps her baby nearby in the room, if not in the bed. When baby wakes at night, mother just nurses the baby and they both go back to sleep. It has been found that breastfeeding mothers have the same biorhythms as their breastfed babies, which means that when a mother is in her deepest sleep, the baby is in his deepest sleep. When baby is in a light sleep, so is mother. Many mothers find they wake just seconds before baby stirs. Mother will probably latch the baby on before he's completely awake, and they will both continue sleeping. In fact, the whole family gets a more restful night. You can see how this is truly an advantage to breastfeeding.

There can be some health benefits for an adoptive mother who is breastfeeding. Many of us know that a pregnancy is a type of rest for our bodies. Pregnancy puts some of a woman's hormones in a semi-resting state. When we can't get pregnant, our bodies don't experience these resting stages. Breastfeeding was intended to naturally follow a pregnancy. Even though periods may not stop as a birth mother's might, an adoptive mother can still experience this cycle and resting stage through breastfeeding. This resting stage of breastfeeding can put some of the related female medical problems in a dormant state. This was one of the reasons my gynecologist encouraged me to nurse my adopted baby.

During the years I nursed my two adopted babies, the cysts and hormone imbalances that I was suffering from went into remission. Other mothers who have suffered from endometriosis have found that breastfeeding can completely put the disease into a dormant state.

During a seminar, one mother asked if there could be a problem for a mother who has an abnormally high amount of prolactin in her system. Sometimes this is a cause of infertility. An abnormal level of prolactin can be a benefit to an adopted nursing mother; however, it is not common. One of the objectives in breastfeeding is to increase prolactin levels, which builds the mother's milk supply. The body will respond more easily if the woman already has an elevated level of prolactin.

When a mother nurses an adopted baby, the new balance of hormones may help correct the previous abnormal hormone levels which were partly responsible for her infertility.

The emotional benefits to both mother and baby cannot be stressed enough. The bonding that comes from breastfeeding spirals down and provides an avenue to meet the needs of the whole family.

A mother can choose to work and breastfeed her baby. The procedure is much easier with an adoptive mother who is nursing her baby and working. She doesn't have the same urgency to pump while she's at work. She can rely at this point more on her supplement device while breastfeeding, even though she will not be building up a potential milk supply as effectively. The time spent breastfeeding her baby before and after work hours can be used to meet the needs of both her and her baby, both emotional and psychological.

The adopted baby goes through a mother-baby separation from his birth mother. There are probably more psychological and/or emotional difficulties due to this than we realize. In some cases a baby might be placed with an intermediate foster care family, before he is placed in an adoptive home. Many times these babies begin to bond in the foster home. This is a sensitive time for a newborn. Another separation (foster-mother/baby) will take place again, when the baby is placed in your adoptive home. These stressful experiences seem to melt away easier and trust is built more smoothly between the mother and baby through the bonding relationship breastfeeding creates.

Breastfeeding can encourage the bonding process between mother and her baby to blossom. Many times mothers feel they are more fulfilled as mothers if they breastfeed their adopted infants. This is especially true if a mother feels unfulfilled because she has not been able to give birth to a child. Breastfeeding provides an element of success for these women. They may feel as though they have failed in some way. Even though this is not failure and is not seen as such by others, this can be the mother's emotional and psychological response. The truth is they can still be wonderful mothers (whether they breastfeed or not), but breastfeeding can certainly help some adoptive mothers to overcome these challenging and discouraging feelings.

Chapter Two

NUTRITIONAL AND IMMUNOLOGICAL BENEFITS

The nutritional benefits of breastfeeding are at the top of the list of advantages. Even formula companies have to state on their cans of formula that mothers' milk is best for the baby. Breast milk is the best food for our babies because it has everything in it, known and unknown, that a baby needs. A breast milk molecule is completely digested in the baby's stomach. Mothers' milk has everything the baby needs, and the baby utilizes almost everything he's taking in. It's so quickly digested that the baby will usually nurse every two to two and one-half hours. In comparison, the formula fed baby ingests a larger molecule which is more difficult for the baby to digest. Therefore, the baby sleeps more because his body has to work harder to digest this formula—not to mention that babies don't even have the enzymes in their bodies to digest these formulas yet (the enzymes are usually not present until the baby is six months to a year old). Soy milk has an even larger molecule than cow's milk, so it can be even more difficult to break down. These molecules can predispose your baby to allergies, with a 25% chance in milk formula fed and a 20% chance of milk allergies in soy formula fed. When we breastfeed our adopted babies, we need to supplement with some kind of formula for the first six months or more. The benefits of having mothers' milk and the flora it provides helps the baby's digestive system.[3]

Mothers' milk contains immunological benefits. Even small amounts of breast milk benefit the baby by providing immunities and preventing allergies, preventing stomach upsets and colic, providing the benefits of facial development, and fulfilling many needs— nutritional, emotional, physiological, sucking, and developmental. Many mothers have heard of the immunological benefit of mothers' milk and how a baby and a mother can come in contact with a virus or bacteria that someone else is carrying around. It's very interesting how the mother's body senses germs she comes in contact with and develops antibodies which are passed to the baby via the mother's milk. The baby usually doesn't get ill at all. (If anything, he might get a light case, but he usually isn't the most ill in the

---

[3]A. Lucas and T. J. Cole, "Breastmilk and Neonatal Necrotizing Enterocolitis," *Lancet* 336 (1990): 1519-1523.

family.) In most cases if the baby is formula fed only, he usually is the one most vulnerable to illnesses. These immunities are there fighting things from the environment that could potentially be passed to the baby. We now know that antibodies in human milk drastically decrease upper respiratory infection and gastrointestinal infections in the breastfed baby. Some pediatricians will even wait to have a breastfed baby immunized until he's older, since the mother's milk provides immunities initially. We know that human milk contains more immunities when we're bringing in the milk supply for an infant. Thus, the immunological benefits increase to compensate for the quantity of milk (more amounts of immunological benefits per unit). The baby gets the best protection possible from his adoptive mother's milk. The quality of the mother's milk is stable, even if the quantity is not provided.

Chapter Three

HORMONES

When a woman is pregnant, oxytocin and other hormones are present (some for the first time) in her body. Even if this woman has a miscarriage very early in her pregnancy, these hormones were present. Since the mother's body will retain traces of these hormones, their pre-existence can be beneficial in building the amounts more quickly when inducing lactation. Even without a pregnancy, some of these hormones might be present in the adoptive mother's body due to her infertility. They may even be the cause of it.

When you begin to prepare for breastfeeding, the first hormone that your body will produce is oxytocin. Frequent and regular stimulation of the nipples sends a message to the pituitary gland that there is a baby at the breast that needs nourishment. The pituitary gland then secretes two necessary hormones—prolactin, which is needed for milk production, and oxytocin, which causes the milk to be ejected from the ducts in the breast. A uterus is not necessary to lactate and breastfeed. The signals are all sent through the pituitary gland (see Fig. 1). However, if the woman still has her uterus, she will probably recognize the presence of the hormone oxytocin by the flutterings felt in her uterus (mentioned also in Chapter 3).

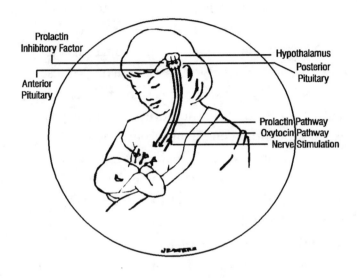

Fig. 1. *Hormone Pathways*

Oxytocin is important in stimulating the milk let-down reflex. Without an effective milk let-down reflex, mothers' milk will not flow easily to the baby, no matter how much milk is there.

The pituitary gland also secretes prolactin. Prolactin is the hormone that causes the alveoli (milk producing cells) to produce milk. If the mom is nursing every two to three hours, milk begins to be made in about four days. Sometime before four to six weeks, the mother should notice a milk "supply" starting to build. Nearly all women have some milk (maybe only a couple drops) after two to six weeks of breastfeeding with proper positioning and frequency, some in four days.

Prolactin is released during times you are nursing your baby or expressing milk. When your body starts to produce prolactin, you will feel its calming influence. I noticed I didn't even raise my voice for at least eight months, and I didn't get stressed as easily. I seemed to stay calm, and because *I* was, my home and family took on a peaceful spirit.

I strongly recommend against drugs that can be prescribed—supposedly to help initiate milk production. The baby's regular nursings alone will send the message to the pituitary gland. Side effects from prescribed drugs can be more of an obstacle than the drug may be of assistance. Most of these drugs create drowsiness or interference with let-down reflex. And there is also a possibility that the drug will be released into the mother's milk.

Although this process of induced lactation sounds easy, there are some underlying factors that can be challenging.

There are some psychological (behavioral) changes attributable to the hormone changes taking place.

There are only mild physiologic (physical) changes in an adoptive nursing mother. These include: milk being produced causing breast changes, including an increase in the breasts' fullness and firmness, sometimes necessitating an increase in bra size.

Note: Breast changes in pregnancy take four to five months. Adoptive mothers go through these stages in a shorter time frame. Pregnancy takes care of the enlargement of the milk ducts, as a rule. In the case of induced lactation, this advantage is absent. The stimulation of an infant nursing at the breast must serve the function of pregnancy for these changes to take place. Thus, hand pumping or hand expression can be further beneficial *if advance notice* of your baby's birth is known. Starting preparation is not recommended if baby is not definite.

Menstrual periods do not vanish as in many birth mothers, but the effects on the cycle can include shorter duration of the menstrual flow and longer intervals between menses (periods). There may be a decrease in the mother's milk supply at the onset of and/or during menstruation. The adoptive mother usually needs to increase the baby's supplement temporarily during this time when her milk supply might be slightly decreased.

Chapter Four

NIPPLE PREPARATION AND CARE

Nipple shells can be an option for an adoptive mother who knows her baby's arrival date in advance. This is common with private adoptions. Instead of pumping prior to the baby being placed, the birth mother can wear breast shells three or four times a day for ten to fifteen minutes; this might induce oxytocin production. Adoption agencies usually don't give you more than a few hours or days advance notice on placement of the baby in your home. This makes nipple preparation and oxytocin induction difficult to do ahead of time. Advance nipple preparation can be helpful. A prospective adoptive mother can begin rolling her nipples between her fingers once or twice a day until she gets notice of the baby's impending arrival. (See Fig. 2 on following page.) This softens tissue behind the nipple and lengthens sinuses to prepare for breastfeeding.

Wearing cotton undergarments allows the nipples to "breathe" and can help discourage thrush (a fungal infection). Leaving the flaps down on your nursing bra exposes the nipples to air and helps them heal more quickly. Be sure that your outer garment (shirt, blouse, or dress) is 100% cotton so air can reach the nipples. Try not to wear an overly restrictive bra (or other clothes) around your breast tissue. The pressure can inhibit milk production, cause plugged ducts, and/or tenderness.

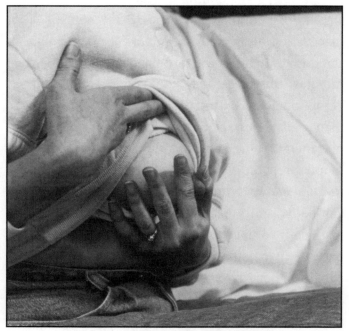

Fig. 2. *Elongating the Nipple*

The advanced inducement of oxytocin, in my opinion, does not often produce mothers' milk. Even when regular nipple preparation is done, there may be some soreness of the nipples when

nursing first begins.[4] If discomfort occurs, I
found the thing that helped me most was aloe
vera, whether you buy it in a bottle or use it
straight from the plant. (Be sure it doesn't
contain other questionable ingredients.) It has a
cooling-healing effect on sore nipples for many
women. It even seemed to toughen the nipple,
which is advantageous. Persistent sore nipples
may have other causes and would need appro-
priate attention to be corrected. For example,
positioning of the baby or the supplemental
nutrition tube could be incorrect. Sore nipples
can be a symptom of thrush, or the mother may
be wearing nylon undergarments next to the skin,
preventing air from getting to the nipples. Air
and sunshine are nature's best remedies for sore
nipples. Vitamin E oil is very healing for
cracked or chapped nipples. But remember, when
apply-ing anything to the nipples, use it sparingly
and apply it gently. The nipples must breathe.

Breast tissue is very easily bruised or injured.
Too much of any product (even vitamin E oil)
will prevent air from getting to the nipples. If
you choose to use a breast cream available on the

---

[4]M. S. Brown and J. T. Hurlock,
"Preparation of the Breast for Breastfeeding,"
Nursing Research 24(6).

to see if it has any ingredients you may be allergic to. Your baby could also develop an allergy to the product you choose. So use caution. If your doctor prescribes medication with cortisone in it, make sure it's cleaned off thoroughly, but gently, before nursing your baby. Aggressive rubbing to remove creams or ointments can further damage an already sore nipple. Some of these medications like cortisone cream can cause serious health problems for your baby, if left on your nipple and ingested. Whenever possible it's best to use a cream that doesn't need to be washed off.

Make sure when your doctor prescribes any kind of medication for you, he knows you are nursing your adopted baby and that you do have milk. Baby can have a serious reaction to a few of the drugs that cross into breast milk. Call a breastfeeding hotline at your local hospital (if available), check with your pediatrician and/or the pharmacist, a lactation consultant, or your local La Leche League to have them check the particular drug you are taking and how it may affect your baby. If the drug isn't recommended while breastfeeding, then you might want to have another consultation with your doctor about an alternative drug that would be safe for a nursing mother. Keep good communication lines open with your physician.

Chapter Five

BRINGING IN YOUR MILK—
YOU CAN DO IT!

When the adoptive mother is bringing her milk in for her adopted baby, it's very much like a newborn and his birth mother. When the infant is first born, the birth mother has colostrum (no milk yet), and in about two to four days her milk will come in. When this happens, she feels like she has milk enough for five babies—much more milk than this little baby of hers needs! But it's not—it's extra blood and lymphatic fluid coming to the breast to help it start working to make milk. This is engorgement. It subsides slowly as the mother's milk supply and baby's needs synchronize.

However, it is a little bit different for an adoptive mother. When she starts nursing her adopted baby, using a supplemental device (Supplemental Nutrition System® [SNS] or Lact-Aid®) (see Figs. 3 and 4 on following pages), in about four days her milk comes in. Her milk is starting to enter the alveoli. She will probably feel a unique sensation that is different with each

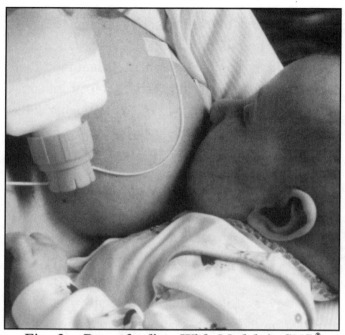

Fig. 3. *Breastfeeding With Medela's SNS®*

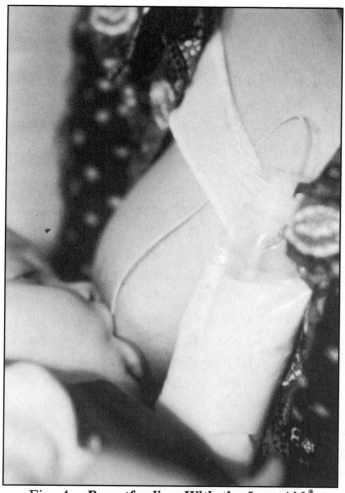

Fig. 4. *Breastfeeding With the Lact-Aid*®

mother. The amounts of milk starting to fill these ducts is different with each mother, too. However, the more relaxed the mother is, the easier it will be to build her milk supply.

Some years ago when my first adopted baby was placed with us, mothers donated milk they had been pumping for their babies who had been hospitalized. The donated milk had quite a bit of colostrum. The colostrum isn't just there for the first four days; for weeks later colostrum is homogenizing with the milk. All of my babies were able to have colostrum because of milk donated to us. Milk is a living organism (with almost as many live cells as blood), and it can carry viruses and disease from the donor. "We know breast milk can actively inhibit and destroy many bacteria, viruses, and fungi; parasites such as giardia and helminths of many kinds—virtually all the potential pathogens the newborn must confront,"[5] as well as provide priceless effects on immune regulation. Receiving milk donations for your baby, if done at all, should be approached very carefully. You will want to screen out smokers and those on medications and drugs.

---

[5]M. Minchin, M.A., "Infant Formula: A Mass Uncontrolled Trial in Perinatal Care," *Birth* 14 (March 1987): 1.

The adoptive mother doesn't produce colostrum. The first few drops of fluid produced is called "pre-milk." The adoptive mother's experience with her milk coming in is different than the birth mother's. Hormone levels and the naturally high prolactin levels which occur shortly after birth cause engorgement. The adoptive mother's milk supply will build slowly. She'll feel tender ducts as her milk starts to come in and can tell perhaps which ducts are starting to get milk. Her milk builds from a few drops to more each day. It might take her a few weeks or a month to get a substantial milk supply, depending on the mother and her body and how quickly her system responds to building prolactin.

Remember, breast changes in pregnancy take four to five months or more. Adoptive mothers go through these stages in a shorter time frame. Hand pumping or hand expression done in advance of baby's arrival (if it is possible to know the baby's arrival date) can be beneficial. Pregnancy takes care of the enlargement of milk ducts, as a rule. In the case of induced lactation, this advantage is absent. The infant suckling at the breast must serve that function of pregnancy for these changes to take place. A mother doesn't necessarily have to have her ovaries or her uterus to be able to nurse an adopted baby. This natural process is accomplished through the pituitary gland (see Fig. 1 on p. 28). When the baby starts nursing at the breast, the sucking sends a signal to the pituitary gland that there is a baby at the breast and he needs nutrition to survive. So the body automatically tells the brain to start making prolactin.

The hormone that starts this whole process is called oxytocin. Regularly scheduled sucking of the infant signals oxytocin production. If the adoptive mother does have her uterus, she might start feeling a fluttering in her uterus. Then she'll know milk production is starting. Of course, when a mother doesn't have her uterus, she isn't going to feel this sensation. These little flutterings in a birth mother are contractions and are beneficial after she has given birth, because they help shrink the uterus back to proper size. Thus nursing is beneficial to help birth mothers get their trim figures back.

When prolactin is first excreted, the mother might notice that she is becoming emotional; she's a lot more sensitive to other people's needs as well as to her own. She might cry over a TV commercial. She may even get discouraged—I try not to call this depression because it's not the same thing. It's not like the "baby blues" that a birth mother might experience after her baby is born; the hormone swing isn't as intense because the hormones present during pregnancy haven't been there. The feeling is more like that exciting high before something special happens or when something really neat happens in your life where you feel a little tearful and a lot more emotional than usual—it's more of a special feeling. But sometimes it can make a mother so emotionally intense she feels maybe she should give up breastfeeding. She starts to have doubts and thinks perhaps it's not going to "work." *This* is the time it is really important that the mother have a really good support system (refer to Chapter 15). The adoptive mother and father need to build that support system in advance. If she has pre-arranged it, people close to her will be saying, "Hey, don't give up—everything is OK." Shortly after this emotional manifestation is when mothers' milk will usually begin to come in.

Prolactin seems to keep your life so calm. The storms in your life seem less intense. People can be arguing in the middle of the room and you sit down and start to nurse your baby. You become a peacemaker. You can feel the prolactin kick in, and the calming effect seems to radiate out to everyone because you seem to have things in control. Nothing ruffles your feathers.

Prolactin is one of the best natural tranquilizers you can ever imagine. It's even been discovered that if roosters are given prolactin, they will mother little chicks instead of attacking them as would otherwise happen. Nothing on the market can touch it!

There are some medications on the market that have been found to produce prolactin. They have been used extensively in severely violent mental patients. When these drugs are used regularly over long enough periods of time, the patients become calmer and their violent nature (part of their mental illness) subsides. These patients can be controlled easier because of these drugs.

In mentally healthy people, these medications are strong tranquilizers—ones that can keep people asleep. I would never encourage drugs to induce lactation. Most medical doctors won't prescribe them for this purpose. A mother needs to be alert and aware enough to take care of herself and her baby. These drugs could interfere with her nurturing ability.

Nor do I endorse the use of synthetic oxytocin that can be prescribed. Syntocinon nasal spray has been used to trigger the let-down reflex but has never been proven to enhance lactation. Ruth Lawrence, M.D., in *Breastfeeding: A Guide for the Medical Professional* states, "Continued use of oxytocin over weeks has been associated with diminished effect or even suppression of lactation." In other words, it has a rebound effect which causes interference with the let-down reflex. There is no proof that this drug helps breastfeeding mothers, and it is speculated that it could be a psychological response.

If you are interested in drug therapy to induce lactation, studies using hormones are being done in Tempe, Arizona, by a doctor who is a fertility specialist. The cost starts at $3,500.

Chapter Six

FORMULA AND
SUPPLEMENTAL SYSTEM

Mothers who are nursing adopted babies need to know how to take care of the formula they put in the supplemental system. The liquid concentrate formula worked best for me, because I could mix it with warm water just before nursing. Ready-to-use formula works well too. The powdered formula leaves a residue that can clog the system. I have tried all the supplemental systems. Fill up the Supplemental Nutritional System® (SNS) or Lact-Aid Nursing Trainer® with formula. Either device hangs around your neck like a necklace and is concealed under your clothes (see Figs. 3 and 4 on pp. 40-41). You can wear the supplementer between nursings (especially if baby is nursing frequently). The formula will be body temperature, as breast milk is when a mother nurses.

Unscrew the portion of the supplementer that holds the formula and clean and/or rinse it between nursings. Reattach it after filling with soapy water and let the water flow through both tubes at once, holding a cup underneath, then rinse with clear water. Do this at least once or twice with soapy water every 24 hours and with clear water each time it is refilled.

I cannot stress enough how important it is to nurse every two hours. If you are concerned about the formula in the supplemental system maintaining its full nutritional value, there is a 1-800 number on each can/bottle that you can call and ask questions.

I called the number and explained the climate and temperature conditions of the area in which I live, as well as the seasonal differences. They told me how the formula kept under each condition including time frames. I would encourage you to call them if you have any questions concerning the formula. Remember, formula will not keep as long in warm weather. You may not want to wear the formula in your unit for long periods of time on warmer days. When leaving home for extended periods of time, a cooler or thermos is advisable for storage. I carried two small thermoses in my diaper bag, one with formula concentrate (chilled beforehand) and the second with warm water to mix it with when refilling the unit. For longer periods of time I had a third one with warm soapy water.

No one can tell a supplementer unit is under your clothing. Each unit was designed to be discreet. The SNS® has two tubes so that you don't have to transfer a tube from side to side when changing breasts (see Fig. 5).

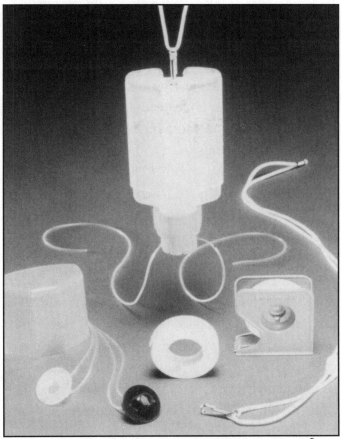

Fig. 5. *Supplemental Nutritional System*®

Both supplementers come with three sizes of tubing—small-medium-large—making it easier to control the flow of supplement through the tubing. Also, the cord that goes around the mother's neck is adjustable. You can control how hard the baby needs to suck to get the supplement from the unit by positioning the device higher or lower. If you have a lazy sucker, this feature can encourage the baby towards a stronger suck. If your baby has a medical problem that causes him to tire easily while breastfeeding or impairs his sucking ability, you can adjust the device to hang high so gravity helps the formula get to baby with little effort on baby's part. This can be effective if your baby sucks quite hard. It encourages them to suck less intensely. It also acts as bait when an adopted baby is going from the bottle to the breast, which is the case in almost all adopted babies. The baby receives immediate gratification, so is more inclined to concentrate on learning to suck properly at the breast, rather than getting frustrated with a new experience. It can meet each mother and baby's specific needs. The supplementer device is effective with handi-capped babies, both for adoptive mothers and birth mothers.

If you use the supplementer at night, make sure the device is in an upright position, even

though you may choose to nurse lying down.
This is similar to a bottle in a position where the
formula is in the base of the bottle near the nipple
so the baby will not get air; the device will allow
air through the tubes if it's not upright. If baby
swallows too much air with the formula, it can
cause gas, colic, and abdominal discomfort to
baby. Don't lay the unit flat or tilted when you
are nursing lying down or reclined in any way.
Keep air from the empty portion of the unit from
getting into the entrance to the tubing (with
formula) at all times. Tuck it between pillows or
something to keep it propped upright, so that it
stays secure vertically (especially if you might fall
back to sleep nursing). Any time that you are not
upright nursing with the unit around your neck,
keep it upright (vertical).

The Lact-Aid Nursing Trainer® is airtight and
will not cause you these concerns. It holds a little
less formula and is a unit with additional pieces
you put together. I recommend you purchase two
of the Lact-Aids® instead of one. Either unit can
be purchased on the order form at the back of this
book.

A mixture of half distilled water and half
white vinegar will remove residue and film that
soap and water alone can't. Rinse with clear
water afterward.

Air in baby's tummy causes pain, so you'll want to prevent baby from swallowing air. If you hear heavy or noisy swallowing, this is probably gulping of air. Check that the supplementer is upright and contains formula. When gulping, baby is swallowing a lot of air with the milk. Slide your finger gently in the corner of baby's mouth to release the suction. Then re-latch baby. Do this each time you hear your baby gulping or swallowing air. You may have to do this with every swallow until baby changes.

Chapter Seven

BREASTFEEDING WITHOUT DIFFICULTY

There are guidelines for a mother who is nursing her adopted baby. Many of them are the same ones that a birth mother would follow for breastfeeding. La Leche Leaders use these guidelines to help mothers avoid difficulties.

To avoid nipple discomfort while you are breastfeeding, make sure baby is latched on correctly. *Breastfeeding shouldn't hurt!* (See Figs. 6 and 7 on following pages.) A good rule of thumb is that if you're nursing your baby and it is starting to get a little uncomfortable for you, unlatch the baby. (The first fifteen to twenty seconds in the early weeks might feel pinchy or painful, but this will go away as the breast gets used to the consistency of nursing.) The best way to unlatch your baby is to slip your finger into the corner of the baby's mouth. Just guide your finger down the breast between baby's jaws so it gently breaks the suction (see Fig. 8 on p. 58). Don't ever just pull baby off or you could injure the breast tissue, causing pain and creating future

Tickle the baby's lip until the mouth opens very wide and the gums go past the nipple. The gums should massage behind the nipple as baby sucks.

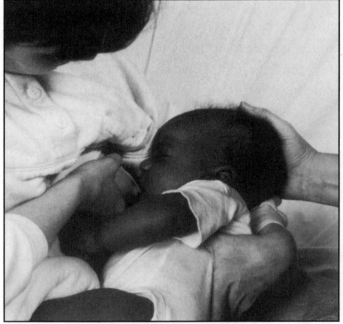

Fig. 6. *Proper Latch-on*

Be sure to center the nipple before baby latches on. Baby's nose should be touching the breast and *will* be able to breathe. Baby's whole body should be facing towards mother.

If it looks like baby's nose is blocked, pull baby's bottom toward you, or lift up on the breast with the hand that holds the breast. Don't press down on the breast with your thumb or it could block the milk or break baby's suction.

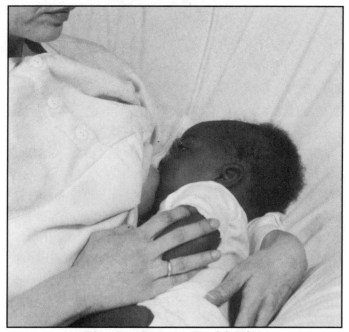

Fig. 7. *Proper Positioning*

CAUTION: (1) Never use cigarette hold to hold breast. Mother's thumb should be on top of her breast and finger beneath. (2) Baby shouldn't lie flat instead of baby's body entirely facing mother. (3) Mother shouldn't hold baby's head but should cradle it in her arm.

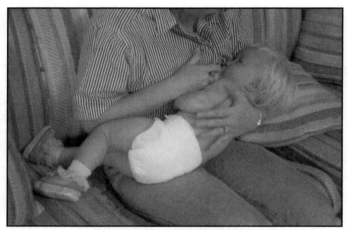

Fig. 8. *Unlatching*

problems. You want to make sure that you're
nursing approximately ten minutes on each side at
a feeding. If the baby isn't satisfied, you can
change to the first side, nursing again on each
side. Make sure baby is properly latched on each
time you switch to the other breast (see Figs. 6-7
on pp. 56-57; also see Figs. 12, 13, 14, 15, and
16 on pp. 77-80). This is called **switch nursing**.

Burping the baby before starting on the next
breast is important and can aid in preventing gas
and discomfort in the baby. The maximum
nursing time frame should be from thirty to forty
minutes. You really shouldn't nurse too much
longer at one time in the beginning, especially
when using your supplemental device. You might

overfeed your baby, because he is getting formula and mothers' milk at the same time.

Switch nursing is beneficial in building a milk supply. This is the technique of breast-feeding on one side, nursing on the other side, switching back to the first breast again and then to the second breast a second time. Some of the benefits are as follows:

1. You're burping the baby several times. Can you see how you'd be doing that? You would nurse the baby on the first side, burp him, then nurse him on the other side, burp him, and then repeat both sides again, burping in between.

2. The baby is a little more active when you're doing this. He's not as apt to fall asleep during the nursing. If all of a sudden you notice baby is slowing down his sucking and starting to doze off or act sleepy, that's when you want to unlatch him, burp him, and move him to the other side. Don't wait until he's asleep. Hopefully, this will keep the baby awake during this nursing time so he will nurse more actively as well as more strongly, which will build your milk supply.

3. Switch nursing causes a series of let-downs that assist in building the milk supply. This is especially helpful when the adoptive mother is inducing lactation.

4. It helps more ducts to work sooner (when inducing lactation).

Ideally we want to nurse our baby every two to three hours, rather than allowing baby to go four hours between nursings. A shorter time between feedings encourages the milk to maintain most satisfactory levels (especially when building the milk supply). If the adoptive mother isn't really concerned about building up a milk supply, she does have the supplement unit as a back up. As long as it's there, the baby can go longer periods of time between nursings. Formula will cause a baby to be hungry less frequently (as discussed earlier in Chapter 2).

If a mother does wish to build her milk supply, it is important to give baby frequent access to the breast. Don't watch the clock. Baby will tell you when he needs you. Nursing every two hours is recommended, more frequently if baby desires.

The first day or so, you will want to monitor how much formula your baby consumes. Nurse as often as your baby wants to breastfeed. Studies show that one-month-old infants consumed 120 KCal/kg per day and the four-month-old group consumed 98 KCal/kg per day.[6] Adjust the formula to encourage baby to nurse every two hours. After the first few days, assess your baby's intake. Breastfeed every feeding with 1/12 of your baby's average daily supplement, so that after 12 feedings in a 24-hour day, your baby has consumed his average intake of formula. If your baby is consuming 725 ml of formula in a 24-hour period, divide that by 12 since you will want to breastfeed every two hours. Fill your supplement device with 61 ml of formula for each of the 12 feedings and breastfeed with that amount at first. When your unit runs out of formula, either continue feeding without a tube or fill the unit with some water (be sure it's not softened water). Increase the formula as needed. Baby needs to be consuming the same amount of formula as previously. He will be nursing more frequently, thus building up your milk supply.

As nursing progresses, the mother will notice baby decreasing the amount of formula he takes because he's now getting breast milk also. If the baby is starting to nurse for too short a time each feeding and/or taking less formula from the

---

[6]C. M. Montandon, C. A. Wills, and A. Garza et al., "Formula Intake of One- and Four-Month-Old Infants, *Journal of Pediatric Gastroenterology and Nutrition* 5 (1986): 434-438.

supplementer, you can increase the fluid in the unit, especially if your baby is one who stops nursing when the supplementer unit is drained. Or you may choose to nurse your baby on the first side without the supplement device (if baby will) and then on the second side with the supplement device. Another key is to watch and see if baby starts going longer than two hours between nursings. The amount of formula may need to be adjusted so baby will nurse more frequently, as close to two-hour intervals as possible.

Water will not hurt the baby, just cause him to get hungry sooner. The goal is to get the baby to nurse frequently enough to build the milk supply, and for baby to still get his caloric and nutritional needs met. Be careful not to use softened water, which is full of sodium the baby doesn't need. Cow's milk formula is already fairly high in sodium.

It is important to be cautious and not cut back on the formula for the baby. Let your baby set the pace. Make sure your baby is having at least six wet diapers a day. You want to be sure baby's caloric and nutritional needs are being met and the baby is gaining weight properly. Don't underfeed your baby.

When breastfeeding an adopted baby, in a sense you are double feeding your baby both breast milk and formula. It's easy to overfeed if you aren't careful. Overfeeding with the formula can create fat cells that will predispose baby to be overweight when he grows up.

If your baby isn't getting enough calories (with too little formula), he will not be as active during nursings. He won't have the energy he needs, even to nurse correctly. He won't be getting the calories he needs to grow and develop brain cells. All of these things are truly important. They are valid concerns of parents. Remember, sucking burns calories. You want to have an even balance. Since you don't really know how much milk the baby is getting at the breast during this time, you have to gauge the amount by how long the baby goes between nursings, how well he is gaining, how active he is, and how long he spends at the breast. The amount of milk really isn't a problem because if there is milk available baby will usually take as much as he needs. For example: if the baby has been nursing ten minutes on one side and ten minutes on the other side, then five to ten minutes on each side again, and then changes his pattern to nursing only ten minutes on the first side and five minutes on the second side, you might guess that baby is getting too much formula. Your milk is increasing and baby is getting full before he's really through nursing. Baby's sucking need has not been met when this happens. Some babies will overfeed to meet this seemingly insatiable sucking need. This is a good example of a time when you might want to nurse only on one side with the supplement device and on the other side without it. Your baby may be one who doesn't want to nurse without the supplementer tube. You can nurse the baby with the tube there and no formula coming through to see if baby will nurse more willingly under those circumstances. Another option would be to use water after the formula is gone (as described earlier in this chapter).

Sometimes baby's tummy just gets full, even with extra water. The same amount of liquid fills him up and he still stops nursing sooner. This baby needs to be encouraged to nurse at least half the time without formula (or water) coming through the supplement device's tube, or without the device at all. Eventually the baby will start to pace himself. He will probably nurse every two hours and get on a schedule himself. Nursing on demand (at your baby's request) is one of the best guidelines to follow to keep baby happy and your milk supply built up.

If a baby is fussy, *nurse!* If he isn't hungry, don't nurse with the device. He may nurse for comfort, relaxation, to satisfy his sucking need, or to meet other emotional and psychological needs. Nursing will not only meet your baby's needs but help build your milk supply. If baby acts hungry or fussy an hour after he's nursed, and he's clean, dry, doesn't need to be burped, and nothing seems to resolve his fussiness, including the colic hold or being put in the baby carrier, he might just need to nurse to meet a need other than a nutritional one. Babies suck differently when they want milk than when they are nursing for comfort. A baby who sucks well can get 80% of the volume of breast milk in the first four to five minutes. Your infant will feed five to eight minutes and sleep for ten to fifteen minutes. The suckling at the breast changes during the rest time.

Many times a baby wants to nurse but doesn't need a complete feeding. He might just need a snack, to suck, or want to be close to mother. Nursing meets all these needs and builds your milk supply at the same time.

Parents need to be aware that babies have growth spurts. Some approximate ages for growth spurts are six weeks and three months. During these times, baby is growing more quickly and will need more calories. To accomplish this, he will nurse more frequently for a few days to increase milk production. Mother may need to increase the formula supplement during these times.

During an adoptive mother's menstrual period, it is common for her breast milk volume to decrease. At this time you may need to increase the baby's formula.[7]

Any time there are changes happening—as during growth spurts or menstrual periods—it is important to relax to encourage the let-down reflex. There are things a mother can do to promote relaxation. Back rubs help the let-down reflex and relax mom. Warm showers, soaking in a warm bath, or applying warm compresses to the breast just before and during nursing can also help the let-down reflex. Breast shells worn for ten to fifteen minutes prior to nursing can be helpful in stimulating milk production and the let-down reflex. However, beware of wearing breast shells "continually" as that can confuse the let-down reflex and diminish your milk supply.

The less you use bottles and pacifiers, the better your milk supply will be; and of course, as

---

[7]J. Lauwers and C. Woessner, *Counseling the Nursing Mother* (Avery Publishing, 1983), p. 94.

was mentioned earlier, it's going to keep baby sucking properly.

Another guideline is to wear cotton clothing—cotton bra, cotton shirt or blouse, and cotton undergarments. If you start having tender breasts, you can drop the flaps of your bra and wear only a cotton T-shirt and let them breathe.

Sometimes, sore nipples can be the result of a yeast infection (thrush). Thrush grows readily in a warm, humid environment such as on covered breasts which get no air to them. It might be the baby that has the yeast infection. Babies can get thrush in their mouths if there was yeast present during their delivery through the birth canal. Babies and mothers are also at risk for thrush if they are taking antibiotics. Sometimes you can tell whether or not your baby has thrush in his mouth if you look inside and see what looks like little white curds of milk on his tongue or inside his cheeks that can't be swept away with your finger.

Are you (the mother) prone to yeast infections? As mentioned earlier, wearing a nylon bra and nylon undergarments can encourage yeast to grow by providing a moist, warm environment. Yeast can be transferred to the nipple by not washing your hands thoroughly after using the toilet or rinsing out a diaper. The yeast transfers to our hands, and then when we touch the breast area to guide the nipple into the baby's mouth properly, we can transfer yeast to the breast and perhaps to our baby. These few precautions can help avoid unnecessary yeast infections or thrush.

If a medical professional does diagnose thrush (also known as *candida albicans*), your doctor can prescribe medication to put in your baby's mouth and for topical use for you. One of these prescription medications is Nystatin.

The Womanly Art of Breastfeeding, third edition, recommends (on page 242) two solutions that can be mixed at home with simple ingredients: water, vinegar, and baking soda. Baking soda is no longer recommended because it can cause high sodium levels and dehydration in babies. The vinegar is mixed with water and used to swab the mother's nipples. This simple home remedy often inhibits yeast growth and corrects the problem when used consistently for several days. These procedures, along with airing the breast, are beneficial in avoiding a prolonged bout with thrush. There are times, however, that this procedure may not be effective. Bathing yourself and the baby separately to prevent cross-infection through the water is a good idea, too. Soda in the bath water is nice.

Don't overlook thrush! It can develop into a more serious breast infection with fevers, flu-like aches and pains, and fatigue as symptoms.

Fig. 9. *Cross-Cradling Position*

Chapter Eight

PROPER POSITIONING

It is important when breastfeeding to hold your baby properly so that nipple soreness does not occur. When nursing on the right side, lay baby across your lap with his head cradled in the crook of your right arm. Turn baby on his left side directly facing the breast. His tummy should be against your tummy. His left arm (the one underneath him) tucks under your right arm, and his other arm can be held with your right hand. Putting a pillow under your right elbow and another under baby to lift him to the height of your breast will help make nursing easier and more comfortable. Pillows also prevent the possibility of bending over the baby, causing back strain and tension. When nursing on the left side, just reverse the instructions (see Fig. 9 opposite).

Make sure your baby is facing your breast when you latch him on. In the correct position the side of his mouth would be at the top of your nipple. It helps to roll the nipple, thus elongating it, before you guide it into your baby's mouth. Holding the breast in a "C" hold with the thumb on top of the breast and other fingers underneath

The mother should first support the breast with her whole hand and place her fingers under her breast, with her thumb on top of her breast. Both need to be placed well behind the areola area.

She should then gently squeeze her fingers and thumb together slightly. This makes the areola area oblong, instead of round. This means that there is now a narrower part for the baby to latch on to.

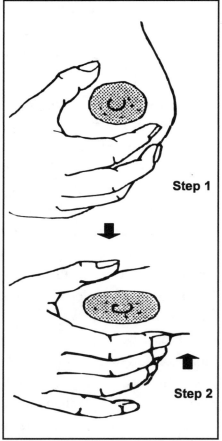

Fig. 10. *Nipple Sandwich or C-hold, Steps 1 and 2*

After making the "nipple sandwich," bring the baby up to the breast, tummy-to-tummy, with the baby coming into the breast straight in (so the baby does not have his head

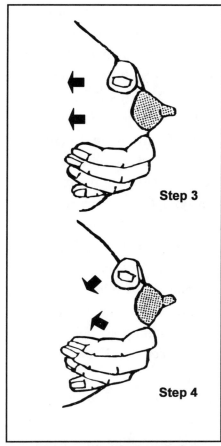

The mother should now push in towards her chest wall or rib. This helps the nipple to protrude further, which makes it easier for the baby to grasp.

The mother should now push in with her thumb more than with her fingers. This makes the nipple point upward toward the roof of the baby's mouth.

Step 3

Step 4

Fig. 11. *Nipple Sandwich or C-hold, Steps 3 and 4*

turned). Pull in as tight as possible; your thumb will keep the breast tissue away from the baby's nose.

and back away from the areola (the dark circular area surrounding the nipple), guide the breast towards baby's mouth, raise the nipple slightly by gently pressing on the breast with the thumb (which positions the nipple towards the roof of baby's mouth), and guide the nipple into the baby's mouth (see Figs. 10 and 11 on preceding pages). These steps make latching on much easier for both mother and baby. Sometimes tickling baby's lips encourages the baby to open wide. You want to get most of the areola into the baby's mouth so that he's latched on and stripping (massaging behind the nipple) properly. If baby is correctly positioned and well latched on, his sucking won't be uncomfortable. This technique ensures that the baby will build your milk supply as much as possible. Correct positioning can also reduce gas in infants.

If your baby is not latched on and just sucking on the end of the nipple, you are likely to get sore nipples. This improper sucking will not build the milk supply, because the baby is not massaging behind the nipple as he nurses. Baby's tongue and jaws massaging behind the nipple gets more milk into the baby's mouth each suck.

Correct positioning is especially important when breastfeeding an adopted baby. As the baby nurses at the breast, the suck-swallow pattern prevents milk from pooling in the baby's ear as it can when a baby is laid on his back or has a propped bottle. When the formula pools and backs up in the baby's ear, it can provide a conducive environment for ear infections. Chronic ear infections and/or recurring ear infections are seen less often in a breastfed baby, due to both the suck-swallow pattern and the immunological benefits of the mother's milk. I am not saying that your breastfed baby will never get an ear infection, only that the possibility of these incidents can be reduced through breastfeeding and proper positioning.

It's extremely difficult to bottle feed a baby in the ideal feeding position. Try to lie on your back and swallow (keeping your head back). It's real difficult. Many times a mother will lay the baby on his back in her lap or in her arms and have baby turn his head sideways towards the breast (or bottle) to feed. This is a frequently seen *improper* position. Try to turn your head with your chin on your shoulder and swallow in that position. It's very difficult. If a baby is lying on his side, with his body in proper alignment, it is so much easier for him to swallow. Proper positioning also helps prevent baby from swallowing too much air.

Not only is it important for the baby to be in a correct position, but the supplemental nutrition system and its tubing must be positioned and used properly. The tubing should be positioned just a little bit longer than the mother's nipple. As the baby begins to nurse, the baby's sucking will elongate the nipple (making it a bit longer); it should eventually be the same length as the tubing. So you will be positioning the tube to be about an eighth of an inch longer than mother's nipple, *before* you guide your nipple into the baby's mouth. The baby latches on around the areola (see Figs. on pp. 77-80).

This is important so I am going to repeat it: *latch baby onto the areola area, not just the nipple.* This ensures that the baby properly massages the area behind mother's nipple, spraying mother's milk up towards the roof of the baby's mouth with each suck. The baby's sucking properly and massaging behind the nipple helps avoid sore nipples and assists in maintaining an adequate milk supply for baby.

Placing the supplementer tube in the proper position as shown and previously mentioned will cause the supplement in the tube to spray in the

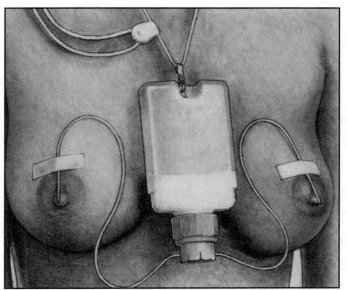

Fig. 12. *Hang the SNS around your neck. Adjust cord so that bottom of SNS is level with nipple.*

same fashion on the roof of the baby's mouth. Baby won't be as likely to chew and tug at the nipple if positioning is correct on both accounts, nor will baby get as much air or be apt to get colic quite as easily. There are many other positions demonstrated in the back of this chapter that are proper and work well. In whatever position baby is placed, be sure he is latched on properly.

1. Position the Nursing Tube tip about 1/4" past the end of the breast nipple, as the nipple will elongate. You may choose to place a piece of tape over the tube at the edge of the areola.

2. Support the breast with your fingers underneath and thumb lightly resting on top, as shown. Do NOT use the incorrect "cigarette" or "V" hold, for the fingers will squeeze together and cause the tube to curl.

Fig. 13. *Right Positioning (Mother Nursing With Medela's Starter SNS ®)*

When positioning tube:

1. Tube 1/4 - 3/8" longer than nipple. (Nipple elongates during sucking.)

2. Tube just off center of lip. Baby in belly-button to belly-button position. Baby's lower arm is underneath mom's arm.

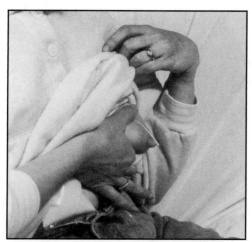

Fig. 14. *Correct Tube Positioning*

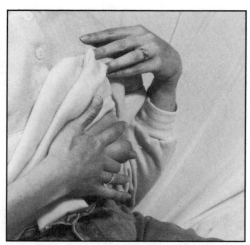

Fig. 15. *Incorrect Tube Positioning*

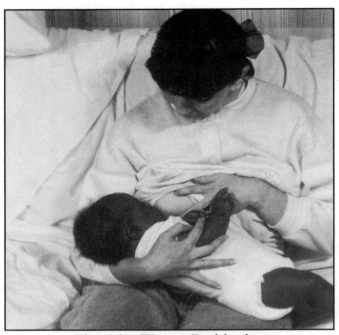

Fig. 16. *Wrong Positioning*

Tube positioned improperly.
Baby in awkward position.

As mentioned earlier, if you're nursing baby on your lap in the cradle hold, it might be helpful to have one or two pillows on your lap to rest baby on and lift him to breast height. Your arm won't get so tired that way. A pillow at your side to rest your elbow can help. A pillow behind your back can be comfortable. A pillow in bed to lay baby on raises him a little higher when trying to nurse on your side from the top breast (or bottom breast with newborns). Medela has a NursingPillow® you can purchase (see order form in the back of this book). Find the position that is most comfortable to you and your baby. Try some of the other nursing positions previously mentioned. You and your baby should be comfortable and relaxed. This encourages proper let-down reflex.

Trying different positions can help you to find the one you enjoy most. Some positions are more comfortable to some mothers than others. Nipple or breast tenderness might be caused from natural circumstances. They occur due to the hormone changes taking place, and because the nipple simply isn't used to a baby regularly nursing at the breast. The nipples get used to breastfeeding after a short period of time. One position that can be helpful to a mother with tenderness or soreness from baby nursing in one position, is for the mother to lie diagonally across her bed, placing a pillow above her shoulder so it is level with her shoulder. She would then lay her baby face down so the baby's feet point in the direction of mother's head. The baby will be facing mother's breast (upside down). Mother will then latch baby on. Not only does this position move the pressure from baby's tongue on the breast to a new location, but gravity pulls baby's tongue into the proper position, and causes baby to latch on to more of the areola, therefore massaging behind the nipple properly.[8] The baby's nose is less obstructed during nursing, and mother and baby are usually very comfortable (see Fig. 17 opposite). If you have sore nipples, breastfeeding in this position can be less painful than in other positions. Mothers who have had a C-section or other abdominal surgery can nurse easily in this position, too.

Nursing in the "football" position is a good trade-off position to the traditional cradle position with baby across your lap. Placing a pillow along either side of you is most helpful. Lay the baby

---

[8]J. Lauwers and C. Woessner, *Counseling the Nursing Mother*, p. 392.

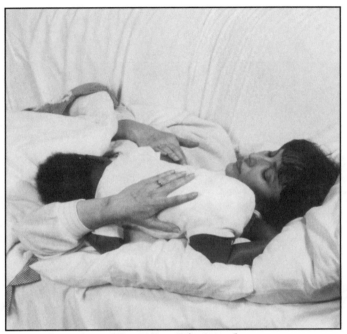

Fig. 17. *Diagonal*

Fig. 18. *Football*

next to you with baby's buttocks next to your back and baby's feet going toward back of the chair you are sitting on—like baby is sitting next to you but facing you. Your baby can be held in a full sitting up position or as reclined as you desire. If reclined, you may want to place baby's legs upward against the back of the chair so baby can't push with his feet (see Fig. 18 opposite). With a younger infant many mothers find that a third pillow on their lap helps. Latch the baby on properly. If your baby is suffering from an ear infection, holding him in a more upright position can be less painful, as well as discouraging pooling of the formula in the ear. The football position has also been known to relieve the discomfort of colic for some babies.

I'd like to offer a few helpful hints concerning your need for a pacifier. Notice I said **your** need, not your baby's need. Your baby will probably never need a pacifier. Pacifiers can be useful, but their use should be limited to *mother's need*. Newborns have an intense need for sucking. When nursing a baby for a long period of time, sore nipples can develop if there is no liquid coming from the breast or supplementer. The baby may have satisfied his nutritional need at the breast but continues to nurse to meet his psychological, emotional, and sucking needs (previously discussed).

The additional sucking on a pacifier can sometimes be a substitute for mother's breast, but *never* a substitute for mother. Hold the baby when offering him the pacifier. Let your baby keep **you** along with the pacifier. As soon as any soreness disappears, baby should once again resume sucking only from mother's breast. Short, frequent nursings can satisfy this intense desire to suck. You can also let your baby suck on your finger with the pad of the finger to roof of baby's mouth (pinkies work well and are most baby-sized). Fingers are always with you and you can't lose them.

The pacifier can affect your milk supply and ultimately the baby's weight gain when you are not cautious in avoiding prolonged use. Babies do not suck properly at a bottle or a pacifier. Your baby might suck improperly at the breast when a habit is developed over a prolonged period of time with a pacifier. Baby may become nipple con-fused switching between the breast and a rubber nipple and may come to prefer a pacifier over breastfeeding and forget to remind you he is hungry. I have seen mothers have to bait their babies into sucking at the breast with the pacifier because of the interference the pacifier has caused.

A pacifier can be a life saver when baby is difficult to calm in an awkward, crowded situation, or if the baby nurses long periods of time, needing to suck to go to sleep. However, I see a common misuse, in my opinion, of pacifiers, when mothers pop the nipple into baby's mouth every time he fusses, not allowing the baby to ever express himself, or to eliminate the need of modifying her routine of duties to meet her baby's needs. **Never forget: you are the one your baby needs!**

If you have a genuine need for a pacifier, I suggest purchasing a one-piece pacifier so there will be no possibility of it separating and the baby swallowing or choking on a piece.

The pacifier only has a use for short periods of time in the majority of cases. By the time your baby is two or three months old, you may find that he will no longer take it, so you won't have to wean him from it later. When you find yourself needing to wean your child from the pacifier, wait until he is two or three years old. When he is not watching, make a small slit in the side of the pacifier. When he sucks on it, it won't work. He'll probably lay it down, go about his business, and return to try a few more times. In most cases he will just give up on it. Suggest that he throw it away because it doesn't work anymore.

Fig. 19. *Lying Down*

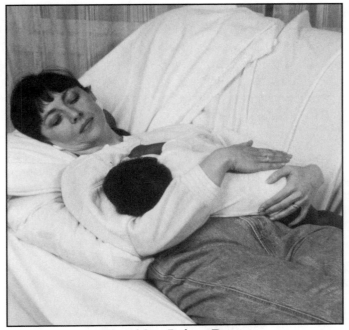

Fig. 20. *Lying Down*

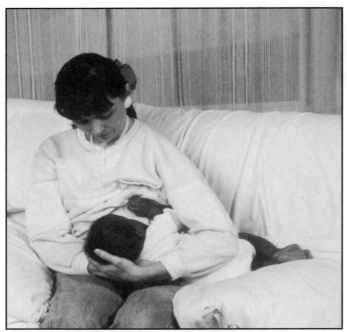

Fig. 21. *Slide-to-Side*

Chapter Nine

TAKING CARE OF MOM

One thing each mother needs to remember, whether she's a birth mother or an adoptive mother, is that in order to take care of her baby the best she can, she needs to take care of herself first. Eat three meals and nutritious snacks each day, so your body receives all the proper nutrients needed to be healthy and happy. At the end of Chapter 12 is a chart to help mother stay within her daily dietary requirements. Sometimes a mother doesn't realize what food groups are lacking in her diet. This is a simple exchange chart with the American Heart Association's diet worked into it, and is used by many doctors and nutritionists.

Get plenty of rest, so you don't get too tired. Drink one quart of water throughout the day. If you are over your ideal weight, add eight ounces of water for each ten pounds you are over your ideal weight. Don't let yourself get dehydrated; your body will not pull fluids from other areas to compensate, thus decreasing your milk supply.

After a short time, you will learn to read your body and "drink to thirst."

A good way to ensure getting adequate fluids is to prepare a drink each time you nurse your baby. If the drink is warm, it may help relax you and encourage the let-down reflex. By drinking a cup of water or other liquid each time you nurse your baby, it is easier to meet your fluid requirements consistently.

Some babies will have a reaction if you are drinking or eating many dairy products. Mothers need adequate fluids but do not need to drink milk to make milk. Stay in tune with your baby's sensitivities. Make sure you are getting a balanced diet and being sensible.

Proper nutrition, adequate fluids, and rest are important for mother's physical well-being. There are ways mother can pamper herself to enhance her emotional health, too. For many mothers, taking a long bath while the father (or someone else) is there to care for baby is relaxing. She may also like to go on a short shopping trip or have lunch with father, an older child, or a friend. Even if baby goes along, the change of scenery and/or companionship can revive a mother's spirits.

At home, mothers often rush to get household duties done while baby is sleeping. It's helpful sometimes to take that time for yourself and read, nap, or work on a project you enjoy instead.

Taking care of yourself physically and emotionally makes you better able to take care of your baby and family.

Fig. 22. *Nursing Discreetly*

Chapter Ten

APPAREL AND
NURSING DISCREETLY

Many mothers ask what the disadvantages of breastfeeding are. (I am not the best source to address this subject, since I am so *pro* breast-feeding.) The mother's wardrobe could possibly be one disadvantage. Every outfit that hangs in your closet would not necessarily be a sensible option for a breastfeeding situation. Nursing mothers may find themselves making some changes in their wardrobe to accommodate discreet nursing. Slacks and skirts with T-shirts and blouses are a favorite. Loose tops are usually the easiest, especially when first starting out.

You can learn to breastfeed your baby without others even being aware of what you are doing. You can be so discreet that it looks like you are just holding your baby (see Fig. 22 opposite; also Figs. 23 and 24 on pp. 96-97).

Front buttoning blouses or dresses are the least discreet types of clothing to wear. At home when discretion is not always necessary, this type of clothing can work.

There are many patterns for nursing fashions, and there are ready-to-wear clothing styles being sold with hide away pockets, hidden open pleats, and other ingenious one-piece outfits created just for the breastfeeding mother. Check your local maternity store, baby magazine advertisements, and your La Leche League magazine.

Practice nursing in front of a mirror. Watch other breastfeeding mothers nurse. La Leche League meetings are a good resource. A La Leche League Leader or member can assist you and give you tips for nursing discreetly.

Fig. 23. *Nursing With Blanket Wrapped Under Mother's Arm*

Remember, many of today's fashions and bathing suits, of course, reveal more of a woman's breasts than breastfeeding does.

Fig. 24. *Nursing Discreetly*

Chapter Eleven

SHARING AND EDUCATING YOURSELVES

Some mothers feel that they and their babies are *too* attached, and they give too much of themselves in the breastfeeding relationship. They feel their bodies aren't their own anymore. They want to be more detached. Many times this is true of a very young mother who still has many needs her-self and is struggling to reach maturity. The thought of a totally dependent baby can be over-whelming. This may also be true of a highly career-oriented woman who has never had to share her life with a totally dependent person. She may feel stress in this new job as a mother. She may feel her career is somehow being compromised. Breastfeeding may seem an overwhelming new lifestyle she must adjust to. Being a new mother is often overwhelming whether you are breast-feeding or not. Breastfeeding may help a mother make this transition more smoothly. Evaluation of your situation and attitude are important. Each mother has a different personality and needs to live within her comfort zone.

Fathers sometimes don't feel supportive of breastfeeding. They may feel baby is interfering and can have strong feelings of being left out or jealous of the baby. This feeling is common and fairly normal. Fathers struggle with sharing the breast with their baby. I've heard my own husband respond to comments other men have made reflecting these non-supportive attitudes. He has asked them: "Do you think they (breasts) were put there just for you?" Obviously, they are not only for man.

Fathers sometimes feel that the baby is taking all of his wife's love and affection. He may feel his needs have taken second place on his wife's priority scale. There is now a baby in the home who is almost totally dependent on his wife. This is a common feeling with husbands.

Don't tune out Dad. If you do, this can cause a major conflict in your marriage relationship.

Discuss your feelings about breastfeeding and parenting with your husband before the baby is placed in your home. Determine if your husband is willing to give full support to you breastfeeding his baby. In many cases this number one position has always been his place (in his opinion). You can reassure him how important he will be and still is in your life *and* the baby's.

In *The Womanly Art of Breastfeeding*, there is an entire chapter dedicated to fathers and their role with their breastfed baby. It has helpful hints on bonding with the baby. I strongly recommend this book. It's inexpensive and educational for the whole family. Encourage father to read through the whole book. Another excellent book is by Dr. William Sears, titled *Becoming a Father*.

Be sure the father and baby have opportunities to interact to encourage bonding. Some examples of activities fathers and babies can enjoy together include taking baby for a walk, especially in a baby carrier, bathing with baby, rocking, reading to baby, dancing and singing, and massag-ing baby. All these activities can promote bonding and create memories.

Chapter Twelve

MOTHER'S NUTRITION

For the adoptive mother who chooses to breastfeed her adopted baby, nutrition is very important. Not only is she "eating for two" and trying to build up her milk supply, but physically she is going through many changes and very quickly. It is the adoptive mother's responsibility to eat wisely in order to keep herself well nourished and healthy. A quality diet will ensure the best milk supply possible for her baby, as well as provide the energy she needs to take care of both her own and her baby's unlimited needs.

Ninety percent of the calories used to make mothers' milk go directly to the baby. The milk production process is very efficient, using only 10% of calories for the body to manufacture the milk. If the mother's body is not provided with adequate nutrition-filled calories, her body will compensate; and she could possibly see a decrease in her milk supply (not in the quality only in the amount).

Mother will burn fat stores during lactation if the body is receiving its nutritional needs to function in good health. If the body's nutritional needs are not met, the body will hang on to fat stores and continue to store calories mother consumes. It will shift into this "survival mode" due to the lack of nutrition being provided to the body.

Women who are not pregnant or lactating need 1200-1599 nutritional calories to meet their bodies' basic nutritional needs. It is recommended that nursing mothers consume an additional 500 calories a day (which should include 20 grams of protein) or a 15% increase over the woman's prepregnant diet.[9] This will provide two-thirds of the body's needs to produce milk. The body will burn its fat stores to provide the other one-third of the body's needs, but only if the body is receiving 1700-2000 nutritional calories, which will meet the mother's nutritional needs.

The Womanly Art of Breastfeeding has a chapter which focuses exclusively on the nutrition of the breastfeeding mother and her family. Getting a balanced diet to provide all the nutritive needs of your body is very important. Educate yourself about the nutritional values of different foods. I've written a little pamphlet (*Vital Attractions*) on nutrients and the foods we find them in. There is information in the back of this

---

[9]J. Lauwers and C. Woessner, *Counseling the Nursing Mother*, p. 113.

book about how you can order a copy. Variety is essential in order to obtain all the nutrients needed from your diet.

Crash diets or fad diets, which encourage rapid weight loss, can be very detrimental to the nursing mother and her milk supply. They rob mother of her milk supply.

A drastic weight loss can alter the mother's metabolism, with the side effect of the body storing fat rather than burning it, since the body's survival mechanism kicks in to protect the body from starvation. When the body is not getting all the nutrients it needs, it cannot burn fat and utilize it in place of nutrients it's not receiving. Fat is toxic waste stored in our bodies. It has no nutrients. The body will store fat and burn lean muscle mass to compensate for the inadequate amount of calories consumed. This is why the body often reaches a state of dis-ease from the stress and neglect, called disease or illness.

It is highly recommended that a breastfeeding mother *improve* the quality of her diet, conscientiously getting nutrients from all food groups. I have provided an easy chart at the back of this chapter. Daily diaries containing charts similar to this one are available as well. I have enlarged this chart and laminated it, added magnets to the back, and keep it posted on the refrigerator for the whole family's awareness.

Mother should steer clear of "junk foods." Junk foods are those foods with empty calories and little or no nutritional value. Good examples are soft drinks and pastries.

If a mother wants to reduce her body fat level, she needs to increase her exercise level. The only way the body will burn fat is when the muscle is heated through exercise.

A breastfeeding mother should never compromise her nutritional needs. Her body will respond to weight loss attempts more readily if her diet is getting the 1700-2000 "balanced-nutritional" calories from the foods her body needs to be healthy and to provide milk for her baby. Good nutrition helps maintain energy level and curtail fatigue and depression. This encourages emotional ups rather than mood swings.

Cutting out the majority of fat in your 1700-2000 calorie intake can, and most likely will, decrease the fat content in your milk. The fat in your diet is 50% of the energy in your breast milk. Eliminating too many fats is not encouraged or recommended for a balanced diet. If your diet fails to provide 30%-40% of dietary energy as fats, your breast milk composition will reflect this in adipose tissue stores.

Watch your baby's responses to what you eat. Some babies may have an intolerance or reaction to certain foods. Chocolate, corn, egg, spicy foods, milk products, and wheat products may be culprits for sensitive and/or allergy-prone babies. If your baby exhibits intolerance symptoms, just eliminate one thing at a time for one week to find the culprit. Sometimes your baby just won't approve of the taste of your food. A few food flavors do go through the milk.

If your baby is allergic to a food in your diet, he may experience colic, eczema, rash, irritability, stuffy nose, or other symptoms. If your baby exhibits any symptom that could be prompted by an allergy, review your diet. Eliminate suspect foods for a short time. The symptom should subside within a week or so. Avoid that food until baby is around one year old. Then try introducing it again cautiously to ensure baby has outgrown his sensitivity.

If you don't see a change in your baby after a couple weeks of eliminating the suspect food, review your diet again. You might want to consult a physician for recommendations.

If your baby reacts to milk products in your diet, consult a physician, nutritionist, and/or dietitian to see if a calcium/magnesium supplement is needed. Your baby should not remain on a cow's milk formula if he has a milk allergy. The wrong formula supplement could be life threatening.

Consult your health professional concerning *your* need for a vitamin-mineral supplement. Don't try to prescribe supplements for yourself.

Nutrients can be obtained from a balanced diet. I have outlined proper portions of each food group at the back of this chapter.

The nursing mother's balanced diet is sometimes considered as one of the magic keys to milk "supply." If she's taking the time and interest in feeding her family and herself right, she usually keeps other things balanced wisely as well.

There are opinions other than mine on this subject.

Adelle Davis, author of *Let's Have Healthy Children*, made popular her "boost-the-milk-supply diet." It features brewer's yeast, milk, liver, wheat germ, blackstrap molasses, and yogurt. I have not tried this combination, and would not, and whether or not it would really work to build "your" milk supply would be different for each mother and her diligence to the other guidelines expressed in my book.

Some concerns I have with all these above suggestions:

1. "Mother's milk tea," an herbal blend designed to build the milk supply, can be traced to the mother's milk, like some drugs, and may or may not be harmful to your baby. Any herb used remedially needs to be considered as a drug and you need to watch for possible reactions and side effects.

2. Brewer's yeast and blackstrap molasses should be introduced to the diet cautiously. Both can cause gas and intestinal discomfort to mother and her nursing baby. The body must gradually develop the enzymes necessary to digest and utilize these products. Only one-eighth to one-fourth teaspoon should be eaten at first as a conservative starting point. I have had mothers report yeast infections for which they felt brewer's yeast could be a contributing culprit. They are both very nutritious foods if tolerated.

3. Of course, milk allergies are a concern with the milk.

4. Wheat germ is a concern if wheat allergies are present. Wheat germ only has its nutritional benefits for a short time after the wheat has been freshly ground. If you are buying it off the store shelf, the nutrients for which you are buying it have lost their potency.

5. Yogurt is a healthy food if you are careful to purchase one with active cultures. Caution should be taken if a milk allergy is present.

Many herb tea drinks are beneficial. Any warm drink may help relaxation and promote good let-downs.

The real key to a healthy diet is informed common-sense nutrition. Maintain your priorities. Don't forget to eat or snack every two hours. Taking care of your nutritional needs helps you to be the best mother you can be.

Note that the printed form uses four columns:

Time:
Write down the time of day each time you eat.

M/S:
This means meal (M) or snack (S). A meal must contain a minimum of 300 calories of wholesome food. Do not skip meals and substitute high-calorie, non-nutritive snacks. Stay away from soft drinks and sweets.

H:
What degree of hunger (H) did you experience before eating? Use a scale of 0-3. (0) would indicate no sense of physical hunger, (1) mild hunger, (2) moderate hunger, and (3) excessive hunger. You are monitoring physical hunger as contrasted to only appetite. A strong urge to eat something is appetite, when you are not actually experiencing physical hunger.

Place:
Where did you eat? Concentrate on enjoying your food. Preferably be undistracted.

DAILY FOOD EXCHANGE RECORD — 2500 Calories

H: In this column note the degree of hunger (H) you experienced at the time of eating. Use a scale of 0-3. A zero (0) would indicate no sense of physical hunger, one (1) would be mild hunger, two (2) would be moderate, and three (3) would be excessive hunger. **M/S:** This means meal (M) or snack (S).

Day of Week_____

TIME	FOOD	H	PLACE	FOOD TYPE AND QUANTITY
BREAKFAST Time_____	Milk (skim) ○ Veg. Fruit ○○ Bread ○○○ Meat (lean) □□ Fat ○○○○ Misc.			
LUNCH Time_____	Milk ○ Veg. ○○ Fruit ○□ Bread ○○○ Meat ○□□ Fat ○○○○ Misc.			
DINNER Time_____	Milk ○ Veg. ○○ Fruit ○□ Bread ○○○○ Meat ○○□ Fat ○○○○ Misc.			
SNACKS Time_____ Time_____ Time_____	250 calories)			

□ = Not required in Pyramid Food Guidelines.

FRUIT EXCHANGES

One fruit exchange includes approximately 40 calories and 10 mg. of carbohydrates.

Apple		1 small	Mango		1/2 small
Apple juice		1/3 c.	Melons:	Cantaloupe	1/4 small
Applesauce (unsweetened)		1/2 c.		Honeydew	1/8 med.
Apricots, fresh		2 med.		Watermelon	1 c.
Apricots, dried		4 halves	Nectarine		1 small
Banana		1/2 small	Orange		1 small
Berries:	Blackberries	1/2 c.	Orange juice		1/2 c.
	Blueberries	1/2 c.	Papaya		3/4 c.
	Raspberries	1/2 c.	Peach		1 med.
	Strawberries	3/4 c.	Pear		1 small
Cherries		10 large	Pineapple		1/2 c.
Cider		1/3 c.	Pineapple juice		1/3 c.
Dates		2	Plums		2 med.
Figs, fresh		1	Prunes		2 med.
Figs, dried		1	Prune juice		1/4 c.
Grapefruit		1/2	Raisins		2 Tbsp.
Grapefruit juice		1/2 c.	Tangerine 1 med.		
Grapes		12			
Grape juice		1/4 c.			

Cranberries may be used as desired if no sugar is added.
Use fresh, frozen, or canned without added sugar.

MILK EXCHANGES

Each milk exchange contains nearly 80 calories, 12 gm. carbohydrates, 8 gm. protein, and a trace of fat.

Skim milk	1 c.
Buttermilk (made with skim milk)	1 c.
Plain low-fat yogurt	1 c.
1% milk (omit 1/2 fat exchange)	1 c.
2% milk (omit 1 fat exchange)	1 c.
Whole milk (omit 2 fat exchanges)	1 c.
Powdered milk	1/3 c.
Evaporated milk	1/2 c.

BREAD EXCHANGES

Each bread exchange contains about 70 calories, 15 gm. of carbohydrates, and 2 gm. of protein.

Bread, any kind	1 slice	**Starchy Vegetables:**	
Bagel, small	1/2	Corn	1/3 c.
English muffin	1/2	Corn on cob	1 small
Hamburger bun	1/2	Lima beans	1/2 c.
Hot dog bun	1/2	Parsnips	2/3 c.
Tortilla	6"	Peas, green	1/2 c.
		Potato, white	1 small
		Potato, mashed	1/2 c.
		Pumpkin	3/4 c.
		Winter squash	1/2 c.
		Yam; sweet potato	1/4 c.

Cereals:		**Prepared Foods:**	
Bran flakes	1/2 c.	Omit 1 fat exchange for the	
Dry cereal, unfrosted	3/4 c.	following items:	
Puffed cereal	1 c.	Biscuit, 2" dia.	1
Cooked cereal	1/2 c.	Cornbread, 2" x 2" x 1"	1
Grits, cooked	1/2 c.	Cracker, butter	5
Rice, cooked	1/2 c.	Muffin, small	1
Popcorn, no fat	3 c.	French fries	8
Cornmeal, dry	2 Tbsp.	Potato chips	15
Flour	2 ½ Tbsp.	Pancake, 5" diam.	1
Wheat germ	1/4 c.	Waffle, 5" diam.	1

Crackers:		**Desserts:**	
Graham	2 sq.	Donut, no icing (omit 2 fats)	1
Matzo, 4" x 6"	1/2	Lorna Doone (omit 1 fat)	3
Oyster	20	Vanilla wafers	5
Pretzels (3⅛" long x ⅛" dia.)	25	Sherbet	1/4 c.
Rye wafers	3	Ice cream (omit 2 fats)	1/2 c.
Saltines	6	Flavored gelatin	1/2 c.
Soda, 2½" sq.	4	Angel food cake	1 ½" sq.
Dried beans, peas and lentils (dried and cooked)	1/2 c.	Pound cake (omit 2 fats)	1/2" slice
Baked beans, no pork, canned	1/4 c.		

VEGETABLE EXCHANGES

Each vegetable exchange contains about 25 calories, 5 gm. carbohydrates, and 2 gm. protein (1 exchange = 1/2 cup).

Asparagus	Greens:	Onions
Bean sprouts	Beet	Rhubarb
Beets	Chard	Sauerkraut
Broccoli	Collard	String beans
Brussel sprouts	Dandelion	Summer squash
Cabbage	Kale	Tomatoes
Cauliflower	Mustard	Tomato juice
Celery	Spinach	Turnips
Carrots	Turnip	Vegetable juices
Eggplant	Mushrooms	Zucchini
	Okra	

The following raw vegetables may be used as desired:

Lettuce (all varieties)	Pickles, dill
Cucumbers	Parsley
Radishes	Watercress

Starchy vegetables are found in the Bread Exchange List

FREE FOODS

Each free food exchange item is 15 calories or less.

Bouillon, broth, Postum, Pero

Gelatin, plain

Pickles, unsweetened

Catsup (1 Tbsp.)

Coffee, tea

Herbs, spices

Lemon and lime juice

Mustard, soy sauce, vinegar

Diet drinks

Sugarless gum, saccharin

Powdered non-dairy creamer (1 tsp.)

Steak sauce

MEAT EXCHANGES

Each **lean** meat exchange includes about 55 calories, 7 gm. protein, and 3 gm. of fat (1 exchange = 1 oz. cooked meat).

Lean Meats

Beef: tenderloin, round, rump, sirloin

Lamb: leg, rib, sirloin, chops

Pork: ham or leg

Veal: leg, loin, rib, shoulder, cutlets

Poultry: chicken or turkey without skin

Fish: any kind, fresh or frozen — 1 oz.

　　　canned fish — 1/4 c.

　　　clams, oysters, scallops, shrimp — 5 or 1 oz.

Cheese: Low-fat cottage cheese — 1/4 c.

Dried peas or beans: 1/2 c. (omit 1 bread exchange)

Medium-Fat Meats — 78 cal./oz. (omit 1/2 fat exchange/1 oz.)

Beef: Lean ground beef (15% fat), rib eye, corned beef (canned)

Pork: chops, picnic ham, Canadian bacon

Liver, Heart, kidney, and sweetbreads

Cheese: creamed cottage cheese — 1/4 c.

　　　　Mozzarella, Ricotta, Farmers, Neufchatel — 1 oz.

　　　　Parmesan — 3 Tbsp.

Egg — 1

Peanut butter — 2 Tbsp. (omit additional fat exchanges)

High-Fat Meats — 100 cal./oz. (omit 1 fat exchange/1 oz.)

Beef: Ground beef, rib roast, club and rib steaks

Lamb: breasts

Pork: Spare ribs, sausage, country-style ham

Poultry: capon, duck, domestic goose

Cold cuts — 1 oz.

Frankfurters — 1 small

Cheese: cheddar type — 1 oz.

FAT EXCHANGES

One fat exchange is approximately 45 calories (1 gm of fat equals 9 calories).

Avocado	1/8	Mayonnaise	1 tsp.
Bacon, crisp	1	Salad dress. (mayonnaise-type)	2 tsp.
Butter	1 tsp.	Almonds	10 whole
Cream, light	2 Tbsp.	Pecans	2 large
Cream, sour	2 Tbsp.	Peanuts, Spanish	20
Cream cheese	1 Tbsp.	Peanuts, Virginia	10
Salad dressing	1 Tbsp.	Walnuts	6 small
Gravy	2 Tbsp.	Nuts, other	6 small
Hollandaise sauce	2 tsp.	Oil, shortening	1 tsp.
Margarine	1 tsp.	Olives	6

SWEETS AND ALCOHOL (100 calories)

Alcohol		**Cookies** (2 small or 2/3 oz.)	
Beer	8 oz.	Brownie	1
Beer, light	12 oz.	Choc. chip	2
Wine, dry	4 oz.	Fig Newton	2
Liquor (not sweet)	1 ½ oz.	Gingersnap	4
		Oatmeal/raisin	2
		Sugar	2
Beverages		Sandwich	2
Lemonade	1 c.	Vanilla Wafers	6
Limeade	1 c.		
Carbonated (sweetened)	1 c.		

Cakes		**Desserts**	
No frosting, white cake	3" cube	Custard	1/3 c.
With frosting (8-9" dia.	1/2 slice	Donut	1/2
2 layered) 1 slice =		Eclair	1/3
1/16 of cake			

SOUPS (10 oz. servings prepared as directed, Campbell's)

Exchange for 1/2 bread and 1/2 meat
Cream of chicken (omit 1 fat)
Chicken and dumpling (omit 1 fat)
Chicken noodle
Chicken with rice
Chicken & stars
Cream of onion (omit 3 fat)
Onion
Turkey noodle
Vegetable beef

Exchange for 1 bread
Cream of asparagus (omit 1 fat)
Cheddar cheese (omit 2 fats)
Manhattan clam chowder (omit 1/2 fat)
New England clam chowder (omit 1/2 fat)
Cream of mushroom (omit 2 fats)
Minestrone (omit 1/2 meat)
Tomato (omit 1 vegetable)

COMBINATION DISHES
Exchange for 1 bread, 1 meat, and 1 fat
Casserole   1/2 c.
Hamburger Helper   1/2 c.
Tuna Helper   1/2 c.
Enchilada   1 small
Taco   1 small
Pizza   1 small slice
Chili con carne w/ beans   1/2 c.
Lasagna   1/2 c.
Spaghetti w/meat   1/2 c.
Macaroni & cheese (omit 1 fat) 1/2 c.

Exchange for 1 meat and 1 vegetable
Beef stew w/ vegetables   1/2 c.
Chicken á la king (omit 2 fats)   1/2 c.
Chop suey w/meat (omit ½ fat) 1/2 c.
Chow mein   1/2 c.

Chapter Thirteen

THERE IS NO ROOM FOR FAILURE

Too many adoptive mothers put the emphasis on producing an adequate milk supply for the baby's nutritional needs. It is more important to focus on mothering, taking care of you, nurturing your baby, and maintaining your nutrition.

Most adoptive mothers *never* produce a completely adequate milk supply. If relying on a supplement for the first six to eleven months is going to concern you, it can be a stress point that sets you up for failure.

Let me share some ideas from my viewpoint as an adoptive mother after breastfeeding my adopted children. Some of my recommendations for a successful breastfeeding experience are:

1. Take care of yourself.

2. Enjoy your breastfeeding relationship and your baby 100%.

3. Eliminate as many of your housework and other responsibilities as possible.

4. Take friends and loved ones up on their offers to help. Let them know how you need them to help out. Encourage a commitment from them, such as a time and day they will help.

Keep your husband involved. Teach responsibility to other children.

5. Mother and baby need consistent, uninterrupted one-on-one time, maybe even to "stay in bed."

6. Nurse frequently and encourage bonding.

7. Take naps and enjoy some kind of relaxation. Your baby *and your body* need pampering right now. Your body is undergoing new developments which will be more stressful if you overdo and neglect resting.

9. When preparing meals, double your recipe and freeze a meal for another day. Simplify meals. Eat naturally.

10. Get involved and stay in touch with La Leche League and other nursing mothers. Their examples and encouragement are inspiring.

11. Baby carriers are great. Baby feels secure next to mother, hearing her heartbeat, feeling her love and warmth. Baby's upright position has the benefits of proper pressure and a gentle bouncing to relieve trapped bubbles and pressures and can reduce colic.

12. Leave your adopted baby in the care of other people only when absolutely necessary and as *little* as possible—for at least the first four to six weeks.

13. Stay relaxed—this helps your let-down reflex and confidence. It's your good mothering through breastfeeding that counts, not your milk supply. Concentrate on your relationship with your baby and taking care of yourself. Your baby will be more relaxed, and you will be less intimidated, more calm, and confident.

14. Practice nursing in different positions. Practice nursing in front of a mirror. Practice builds confidence and your skill at nursing discreetly anywhere.

15. Always roll your nipple before latching your baby on.

16. Invite others to give you a back rub (or just shoulders and neck) before or during nursing for relaxation.

17. Stay clear of people who offer negative advice or comments. They may mean well, but comments like, "Do you *really* have enough milk?" or "Is he gaining weight?" or "Why are you doing this?" are not what you need. Comments like, "We've both been doing great!" and "This has been truly a special experience!" need to always be kept ready.

Remember that we are building a love-trust relationship with our babies. Time and touching are the language of this relationship. The time you invest pays off with a mother/baby bond almost beyond imagination. Great bonuses include building your milk, a calm, happy baby, more restful nights, and a content family.

If baby is missing his foster mother or birth mother, rock him, nurse him if he'll nurse, talk to him, stroke him, or take a warm, relaxing candle-light bath with him. A gentle baby massage might help too.

If baby refuses the breast or struggles at the breast (confused and frustrated), don't make it a miserable learning experience. After five minutes spoon feed him or use an eye dropper so he doesn't get too hungry. Or let the tube just drip into his mouth. *Don't offer a bottle or other nipple substitute such as a pacifier.*

My daughter was a month old when we got her. The first thing I did was run a warm bath for both of us and got in the bath with her. I ran my hands gently along her body and then snuggled her to my breast. She latched on very relaxed. It took a few minutes for her to suck right, for she had been sucking at a bottle with a regular nipple. Her suck would make a popping sound because she was confused about where to place her tongue.

I introduced her to the supplement tube, when we switched to the other side. She always loved nursing in the bath. Most babies do. Many babies will nurse in the bath if they are resisting the change from bottle to breast.

Also, if baby's resisting, try nursing him while he's asleep. Many babies will nurse instinctively in their sleep.

By withholding bottles and pacifiers, baby will eventually need to suck. Sucking is a *need* that must be met. If you continue to spoon feed and/or use an eye dropper, you'll quickly find that baby wants to learn to suck at the breast.

Approximately 63%-75% of babies under three months old have a positive reaction to the breast. Some babies take time to teach to nurse, even with their birth mothers. This is normal. The assistance of a local La Leche League Leader or other lactation consultant can be very helpful.

Any adoptive mother can have a rewarding breastfeeding experience and develop a warm and loving bond between her and her baby, even if she doesn't produce her own milk supply. The quantity of her milk supply should *never* be her motivation.

Chapter Fourteen

WEANING

Weaning your adopted baby can be one step or as many as four steps. You may choose to wean your baby from the supplement device, and then later baby will wean himself from the breast. This requires weaning the baby twice.

If you wean the baby too early from the breast and he still has sucking needs, you need a sucking substitute such as a bottle and/or pacifier. This requires an eventual third and/or fourth weaning.

Your baby needs to be weaned from the bottle and then at a later time, from the pacifier, if both sucking substitutes are introduced. It is not recommended that baby be weaned from both at the same time.

The weaning process technically begins when the baby is introduced to solids around six months old. When you get that inevitable flack about weaning from well meaning friends and loved ones, you can, at this time, tell them you have begun.

Some cues to watch for that will indicate that your baby may be ready for solids are: his breastfeeding demand will suddenly increase considerably, and/or he'll exhibit a readiness to chew by grabbing anything on the way to mouth of whoever is holding him. If the baby is less than six months old, there are many other causes for these behavior patterns: illness, teething, unusual tension in his environment, and/or any special need for extra comfort.

If your child begins to show these signs, wait a few days and see if these cues vanish or the other concerns listed above become apparent. If these signs persist, after you have breastfed your baby, try your baby on a quarter-teaspoon of mashed ripe banana, avocado, or papaya. If he doesn't push it out of his mouth in disgust and seems to enjoy it, then he's probably ready for solids! If he isn't interested in food the first few times, discontinue offering for another week. Never coax or persuade your baby or child, or force him to eat.

Introduce only one new food at a time, with a space of a week in between new foods, watching for allergic reactions. Slowly increase the amount from quarter-teaspoon.

Many mothers find it is much easier to breastfeed baby until the baby himself is ready to wean. This is referred to as baby-led weaning.

If you are not always using the supplemental device when your baby nurses, you may find at some time after your baby is six months old that he happily nurses on both sides without the supplementer device. You may at that time wish to eliminate the device one nursing each day, until you are no longer using the device. You may want to make this transition even more slowly if baby seems to object.

Some babies will not want to wean from the device. It represents part of the nursing relationship to them: sensations, feelings, and taste your baby identifies with breastfeeding. If your baby is one of those who wants the nutritional supplement to remain part of the breastfeeding relationship, try to comply without reservation. It is all right for the device to be there. The sooner you adopt that attitude, the smoother you and your baby's breastfeeding relationship will be.

When your baby is ready to wean from the breast entirely, you will see many signs. He will be easily distracted by the world around him and when he is busy, he will skip nursings. You can offer him a glass of his favorite beverage, a story, or one of his other favorite things in place of nursing, and he will concede. Then slowly eliminate nursings one at a time: one every few days or every few weeks, depending on how smooth the transition seems and how cooperative the child is. Your child will be the one to eliminate the last nursing in most cases, and he will do it of his own free will—believe it or not.

Chapter Fifteen

INFORMATION AND SUPPORT

The body's ability to make milk in the absence of giving birth is a concept that eludes many adoptive mothers. Many doctors and other health care professionals do not avail themselves of this information, due to a lack of interest and/or time.

A doctor's profession demands an enormous amount of time to help patients regain or maintain quality health. A doctor could spend many hours sharing information with a breastfeeding mother to help avoid or smooth out difficulties, or he could refer her to a La Leche League Leader for ongoing, long-term support, counseling, and information, or to a lactation consultant for crisis intervention. Referring the mother to someone who specializes in breastfeeding management is helpful in making time available for others' needs in his practice. Since management problems rarely require costly medical attention, this referral is less expensive for the breastfeeding mother.

All La Leche League Leaders and most lactation consultants are women who have breastfed their children. Some may be health care professionals. They work exclusively with breastfeeding mothers and can easily identify with them. Their knowledge and experience helps them relate to nursing mothers. Doctors appreciate the time and effort spent by La Leche League Leaders and lactation consultants to help and counsel these mothers.

La Leche League Leaders and lactation consultants have a great reservoir of educational information for mothers interested in breast-feeding. La Leche League International (a non-profit group) offers the help and support of Leaders and monthly group meetings throughout the United States and in 47 other countries.[10]

As mothers contemplate the possibilities of nursing their adopted infant and begin to educate themselves, I strongly recommend that they seek out the La Leche League[11] group in their area and attend meetings for education and enrichment, and most of all for the support. Through these meetings and associations, you can gain an understanding of some of the mothering concepts and techniques that make breastfeeding a

---

[10]The La Leche League International Resource and Info Hotline number is 1-800-525-3243.

[11]A La Leche League membership can be purchased on the order form in the back of the book.

rewarding and positive experience for both mother and baby.

I recommend reading the book *The Womanly Art of Breastfeeding* from La Leche League. It's a handbook for the breastfeeding mother that answers just about any question she has concerning breastfeeding, the breastfed baby, and the family. When she has questions and concerns and wonders if things are normal, or how to handle different situations, there are ready references throughout the index to any subject, including how parents can help siblings be more accepting of the new baby, sexuality, nutrition, fun things for fathers to do to get involved, and many special situations. This book is the best resource I've found for both parents' interest in breastfeeding.

Being educated prior to receiving the baby is much more beneficial, even when preparing to do something as seemingly easy and natural as breastfeeding your baby. The more prepared and educated you are, the more successful you can be, because you will be more confident and informed. If time permits, read other books on parenting and breastfeeding. *Nursing Your Baby* by Karen Pryor is another good selection. Dr. William Sears, a world renowned pediatrician, has written many books which I strongly recommend. Your local La Leche League group may have Dr. Sears' books in their lending library or have new copies to purchase. Your local library may also carry these books.

Your local La Leche League Leader is qualified to assist you and is a source of support and information. She can provide you with additional information concerning breastfeeding. I encourage you to attend the LLL meetings nearest you. Encourage a friend to go with you if you're apprehensive about going alone. You will find many friendships and a wealth of support in your local La Leche League group meetings.

Never let your motivation to breastfeed be the quantity of milk you produce. Stress over your milk supply will discourage you and can suppress the building of your milk supply. If the amount of milk you have or how quickly you can build your milk supply is a strong motivator and priority to you, I would discourage you from nursing your adopted baby.

Talk openly to friends and relatives about your goal to breastfeed your adopted baby. Express the importance of their support. Tell them you are "counting" on their support and ask them never to discourage you. Give them ideas for positive comments to encourage you when you need it most. Explain the process and tell them how their positive attitudes and support can strengthen and sustain your efforts. Most importantly, discuss parenting and breastfeeding with your husband and be sure you have his complete support. Without him as confidant and advocate, it will be easy to become discouraged and possibly fail.

Not only does the adoptive mother prepare her body physically to nurse, she needs to prepare herself emotionally and psychologically, which might be more important, more time consuming, and more difficult than the physical preparation. We need to remember that the birth mother in comparison has had nine months to prepare physically, emotionally, and psychologically.

Do some serious physician shopping (for either a family physician and/or pediatrician and/or gynecologist). Talk with lots of other breastfeeding mothers who share your ideals. You need to find your family or family-to-be a very supportive, sensitive, open-minded physician(s) with whom you can communicate and trust.

SUGGESTED READINGS

Applebaum, R. M. *Abreast of the Times*.
Miami: Applebaum, 1969.

Auerbach, K., Ph.D. and J. L. Avery. *Nursing
the Adopted Infant: Report from a Survey*,
Monograph no. 5, 1979.

Avery, J. L. *Induced Lactation: A Guide for
Counseling and Management*. Denver: J. J.
Avery, Inc., 1973.

Brewster, D. P. *You Can Breastfeed Your Baby*.
Rodale Press, 1979.

Crook, W. G. *The Yeast Connection: A Medical
Breakthrough*. Professional Books, 1984.

Davis, A. *Let's Have Healthy Children*. The
New American Library, Inc., 1972.

Dewey, K. G., et al. *Growth of Breastfed and
Formula Fed Infants 0-18 months: The
DARLING Study*. ARTS Biomedical, 1990.

Fisher, G., E. Parent, and D. Remington. *How
to Lower Your Fat Thermostat*. Vitality
House International, Inc., 1983.

Hormann, E. "Breastfeeding the Adopted Baby."
Birth and Family Journal 4 (1977): 165.

Kleinman, R., et al. "Protein Values of Milk
Samples from Mothers Without Biologic
Pregnancies." *Journal of Pediatrics* 97
(1980): 612.

Kutner, Linda. "Care Plan for Thrush." *Journal of Human Lactation* 2, no. 2 (Sept. 1986): 76-77.

La Leche League International. *The Breastfeeding Answer Book.* Franklin Park, Illinois: La Leche League International, 1991.

La Leche League International. *The Womanly Art of Breastfeeding.* Franklin Park, Ill.: La Leche League International.

Lauwers, J. and C. Woessner. *Counseling the Nursing Mother.* Avery Publishing, 1983.

Lawrence, R. *Breastfeeding: A Guide for the Medical Profession.* St. Louis: C. V. Mosby, 1980.

Montagu, A. *Touching: The Human Significance of the Skin.* New York: Columbia University Press, 1971.

Montandon, C. M., C. A. Wills, and A. Garza, et al. "Formula Intake of One- and Four-Month-Old Infants. *Journal of Pediatric Gastroenterology and Nutrition* 5 (1986): 434-438.

Neifert, M. R. and M. C. Neville. *Lactation, Physiology, Nutrition and Breastfeeding.* New York: Plenum Press, 1983.

Newton, M. *Milk: The Mammary Gland and Its Secretion*. Kon & Cowie, Eds. New York: Academic Press, 1961.

Prentice, A. and A. Prentice. *Maternal Energy Requirements to Support Lactation*. ARTS Biomedical, 1990.

Riordan, J. *A Practical Guide to Breastfeeding*. St. Louis: Mosby Co., 1982/1984.

Zimmerman, M. A. "Breastfeeding the Adopted Newborn." *Pediatr Nurs* 7, no. 1 (Jan.-Feb. 1981): 9-12.

If you desire a complete list of references, contact the author at 1731 Swan St., Ogden, Utah 84401. I would be glad to send a copy.

INDEX

The Author and Her Family

ABOUT THE AUTHOR

Debra has been speaking in classes, seminars, and workshops to adoption groups, health depart-ments, Women, Infants, and Children (WIC), and hospitals for fourteen years on breastfeeding, child care, the child's self-esteem, and breastfeeding the adopted baby. Debra and her husband David have three breastfed adopted children.

As the owner of the Body Profile Clinic, she does lactation consultation and breastfeeding product sales. Debra has counseled adoptive mothers on breastfeeding for over twelve years. She is a La Leche League Leader and Assistant to the professional liaison in Utah La Leche League.

Debra has worked with a local adoption agency for six years as a social aide doing home studies, interims, counseling, speaking, and classes. She and her husband directed an educational enrichment seminar program at the local hospitals for LDS Social Services.

Debra has also served on the State Adoption Board for seven years and the WIC Health Advisory Board for five years in Utah.

ORDER FORM

QTY	ITEM	EACH	TOTAL
	SNS	32.00	
	Starter SNS	12.50	
	Hand Pump	24.95	
	Mini Electric Breastpump	77.40	
	Breast Shells	9.70	
	Disposable Bags for Milk	17.85	
	NursingPillow®	29.95	
	Haberman Feeder (bottle)	16.00	
	Lact-aid Nursing Trainer Kit	38.00	
	Dr. Mom, A Guide to Baby and Child Care, by Marianne Neifert	9.95	
	The Womanly Art of Breastfeeding by La Leche League International	9.95	
	La Leche League Membership (no shipping if ordered alone)	30.00	
	Adoptive Mother's Resource List (no shipping if ordered alone)	1.00	
	The Breastfeeding Triad (including Father)	1.00	
	Breastfeeding Your Adopted Baby by Debra Stewart Peterson	8.95	

Please send my order to:

Name: _____

Address: _____

_____

_____

Phone: _____

Sub Total	$
Sales Tax **6½%**	
Shipping	
GRAND TOTAL	$

Phone Orders with VISA or MasterCard accepted
1-801-392-9074

Send order to:
BPC ● P.O. Box 1736 ● Ogden, UT 84402
Please allow 6-8 weeks for delivery

¿Quién fue
Ana Frank?

¿Quién fue
Ana Frank?

Ann Abramson
Ilustraciones de Nancy Harrison

Altea

Santillana USA

A la memoria de todos los niños, como Ana,
cuyas vidas se truncaron en aquella terrible guerra.
A. A.

Altea

Título original: *Who Was Anne Frank?*
© Del texto: 2007, Grosset & Dunlap.
© De las ilustraciones de interiores y de portada: 2007, Nancy Harrison
Todos los derechos reservados.
Publicado en español con la autorización de Grosset & Dunlap,
una división de Penguin Young Readers Group.

© De esta edición:
2009, Santillana USA Publishing Company, Inc.
2023 NW 84th Avenue
Miami, FL 33122, USA
www.santillanausa.com

Altea es un sello del **Grupo Editorial Santillana**. Éstas son sus sedes:

ARGENTINA, BOLIVIA, CHILE, COLOMBIA, COSTA RICA, ECUADOR, EL SALVADOR, ESPAÑA,
ESTADOS UNIDOS, GUATEMALA, MÉXICO, PANAMÁ, PARAGUAY, PERÚ, PUERTO RICO,
REPÚBLICA DOMINICANA, URUGUAY Y VENEZUELA.

¿Quién fue Ana Frank?
ISBN: 978-1-60396-429-6

Printed in U.S.A.

15 14   2 3 4 5 6 7 8 9

Índice

¿Quién fue
Ana Frank?

La vida de Ana fue corta. Cuando murió, en 1945, tenía tan sólo 15 años. Nació en Alemania, donde la familia de su padre había vivido durante mucho tiempo.

Su padre se sentía muy orgulloso de ser alemán. Estaba seguro de que sus hijos, y los hijos de sus hijos, vivirían en Alemania.

Sin embargo, eso nunca sucedió. La vida de los Frank dio un giro enorme. Tuvieron que huir de su país. Tuvieron que esconderse. Perdieron todo lo que atesoraban… todo, porque eran judíos, y porque un hombre llamado Adolfo Hitler llegó al poder.

Hitler odiaba a los judíos. A *todos* los judíos. Cuando Hitler fue derrotado, ya había muerto la mamá de Ana. También Ana y su hermana. La única persona de la familia que sobrevivió fue Otto, el padre de Ana, a quien ella tanto amaba.

Hubo otra cosa que sobrevivió: el diario de Ana. Ana escribió en su diario durante los dos años en que su familia estuvo escondida. Se escondían de los soldados de Hitler.

Ana comprendió los peligros que enfrentaba su familia. Aun así, lo que escribió en su diario estaba lleno de esperanza acerca del futuro del mundo, a pesar de que estaban ocurriendo cosas espantosas. Ana buscó consuelo en la belleza de la naturaleza, a pesar de que no podía salir ni siquiera para tomar una sola bocanada de aire fresco. Después de su muerte, su diario se convirtió en un libro.

EL DIARIO DE

ANA FRANK

ADOLFO HITLER

Adolfo Hitler nació en 1889. Al comienzo quería ser artista, pero no tenía suficiente talento. Entonces decidió meterse en la política. Soñaba con convertir Alemania en el imperio más poderoso de la tierra. En alemán, "líder" se dice *führer*, y era así mismo, *führer*, como los alemanes llamaban a Hitler.

Hitler gobernó Alemania entre 1933 y 1945 cuando, al final de la Segunda Guerra Mundial, decidió quitarse la vida en lugar de rendirse y enfrentar un juicio.

Desde el comienzo, Hitler convenció a los alemanes de que los judíos eran los culpables de todos los problemas del país. En sus discursos, agitaba a la multitud gritando que había que hacer algo al respecto. Su respuesta era que había que deshacerse de los judíos, de todos ellos. Como resultado, se mató a 13 millones de personas; 6 millones eran judíos.

¿Cómo puede alguien ser tan malvado? Desde la muerte de Hitler, se han escrito miles de libros sobre él. Sin embargo, ninguno ha encontrado la respuesta.

Hoy, más de 60 años después de la última fecha que aparece en su diario, Ana sigue siendo considerada un símbolo de esperanza. Su diario se ha traducido a más de 65 idiomas. Se han vendido más de 30 millones de copias. Se han hecho películas y obras de teatro sobre su vida.

Una corta vida —incluso una muy corta— puede estar repleta de significado.

Capítulo 1
Un hogar feliz

Ana Frank nació el 12 de junio de 1929 en la ciudad de Frankfurt, en Alemania. Doce días después, la pequeña bebita y Edith, su madre, dejaron el hospital y llegaron a casa.

Los Frank eran como muchas otras familias de la época. Otto, el padre, era un hombre de negocios. La madre se quedaba en casa cuidando a Ana y a Margot, su hermana mayor.

Los Frank llevaban una vida cómoda. La señora Frank tenía la ayuda de una niñera. Tenían buena ropa y comían bien. Ana tenía su propio arenero para jugar. El apartamento en el que vivían en Frankfurt estaba repleto de libros.

Otto Frank era varios años mayor que su esposa. Eran lo opuesto en muchas cosas. Él era alto y delgado. Ella era rolliza. A él le gustaba estar rodeado de gente. Era alegre y extrovertido. Ella era tímida y callada.

A Otto le encantaba leerles a sus hijas. También inventaba maravillosas historias a la hora de dormir. Algunas historias eran acerca de dos hermanas llamadas Paula. Una de las Paulas era bien educada y se comportaba bien, como Margot. La otra Paula siempre se estaba metiendo en problemas. Se parecía más a Ana, que era muy traviesa.

Las dos niñas adoraban a su papá. Lo apodaban "Pim". Además de contar historias, a Pim también le gustaba jugar. Además, era un muy buen fotógrafo. Les tomó muchas fotos a las niñas y tenía un álbum para Ana.

Ana también era muy cercana a su abuela, a quien llamaban "Oma". A Oma le encantaba mimar a Ana. Un día, al subir a un autobús con Oma, Ana dijo, mirando a los pasajeros: "¿No hay nadie que le ceda su asiento a esta anciana?". ¡Ana tenía tan sólo 4 años y medio! Ésa era Ana. No tenía pelos en la lengua.

Su padre la comprendía. Él y Ana se parecían
mucho. Sin embargo, Ana no se llevaba igual de bien
con su madre. Peleaban con frecuencia. Ana sentía

celos porque pensaba que su hermana era la favorita de su madre. Margot era seria y de buenos modales. Ana, en cambio, era temperamental y tenía mal genio. Pero también era animada y divertida. Ambas tenían un lustroso cabello oscuro, ojos grandes y una hermosa sonrisa.

Los Frank eran judíos. Observaban ciertas costumbres e iban a la sinagoga a orar en días especiales. Celebraban algunas de las fiestas judías; no todas. Había algunas costumbres judías que no seguían.

Muchos de los amigos que Ana y Margot tenían en el vecindario no eran judíos. A veces iban a la casa de los Frank a celebrar fiestas judías, como Hanukkah.

Menora de Hanukkah

Como sucede con todos los niños pequeños, Ana no era totalmente consciente de lo que sucedía en el mundo exterior a su entorno. Conocía su casa, su familia y sus amigos. Ése era su mundo. No sabía que muchas cosas estaban cambiando en Alemania, y algunos de esos cambios eran terroríficos.

La Primera Guerra Mundial había terminado en 1918 con la derrota de Alemania. Contrario a lo que pasaba con Otto Frank, muchos alemanes no tenían trabajo. Además, los precios de todo —incluyendo la leche y el pan— estaban por los cielos.

Un nuevo líder subió al poder en 1933: Adolfo Hitler. Era la cabeza del partido Nacional Socialista, o Nazi. Hitler ayudó a los alemanes a sentirse mejor acerca de sí mismos. Les dijo que los alemanes eran más inteligentes y mejores que el resto de la gente que habitaba el planeta. Los "alemanes puros", por supuesto. No los judíos. En sus discursos frente a grandes multitudes, Hitler culpaba a los judíos de todos los problemas de Alemania.

La Primera Guerra Mundial

La Primera Guerra Mundial, también llamada "la Gran Guerra" fue un terrible conflicto que duró de 1914 a 1918. Las Potencias Centrales (Austria, Hungría, Alemania y Turquía) lucharon contra los Aliados (Rusia, Gran Bretaña, Bélgica, Italia, Francia y, más tarde, Estados Unidos).

Al final, ganaron los Aliados. Se obligó a Alemania a pagar mucho dinero en castigo por el papel que jugó en la guerra. Esto dejó al país muy pobre y a gran parte de sus habitantes llenos de resentimiento. Se instauró una nueva forma de gobierno —la democracia—, pero no era muy fuerte. En 1933, los alemanes esperaban que Adolfo Hitler, un peligroso líder, ayudara al país a recuperar su grandeza.

A la Primera Guerra Mundial también se le llamaba "la guerra que terminará con todas las guerras". Lamentablemente, no fue así. La Segunda Guerra Mundial comenzó tan sólo 20 años después.

Antisemitismo quiere decir "odio a los judíos". Ya había antisemitismo en otros lugares, aparte de Alemania, antes de Hitler. En todo el mundo, en diferentes momentos históricos, los judíos habían tenido que vivir en vecindarios especiales. No podían asistir a las mismas escuelas a las que iban los cristianos, ni podían tener ciertos trabajos.

Sin embargo, Adolfo Hitler fue más lejos. Su plan era deshacerse de todos los judíos. Por supuesto que

no lo dijo en voz alta. Al menos, no al comienzo. Pero desde el día en que asumió el poder, comenzó a complicarles la vida a los alemanes judíos, como la familia Frank.

Hitler era peligroso. Otto Frank lo vio con claridad. Decidió que su familia estaría a salvo si dejaban Alemania. Debió ser muy difícil para el padre de Ana el tomar la decisión de dejar su hogar. Otto amaba su país. Había luchado por Alemania en la Primera Guerra Mundial. En 1933 había más de 500,000 alemanes judíos. Durante los siguientes seis años, más de la mitad huyó del país.

Por un corto tiempo, vivieron en Suiza con una de las abuelas de Ana. En el otoño de 1933, Otto Frank se mudó a Amsterdam. Para enero de 1934, el resto de la familia se había mudado allí también.

Amsterdam es la ciudad más grande de Holanda, un pequeño país al oeste de Alemania. ¿Por qué los Frank escogieron este país? Primero, porque estaba cerca. Además, Otto ya hablaba holandés. La razón más importante, sin embargo, era que los holandeses eran famosos por llevarse bien con todo el mundo, incluyendo a los judíos.

En Amsterdam, Otto montó una nueva compañía. Fabricaba pectina, un polvo que se usa para hacer mermelada. Los Frank se mudaron a un apartamento en un sector de nuevas viviendas. Las niñas comenzaron a ir a la escuela. Hicieron nuevos amigos. Muy pronto, aprendieron holandés. La única que tuvo dificultades con el nuevo idioma fue Edith. Siguió hablando alemán y esto la hacía sentirse fuera de lugar en Holanda. A pesar de todo, Otto creía que su familia estaba a salvo de Hitler. Estaba equivocado.

Capítulo 2
Un nuevo hogar

Amsterdam es una bonita ciudad. La atraviesan varios canales. A todas horas, van y vienen barcos por esos canales. Cuando se mudó allí, en 1934, Ana tenía tan sólo 4 años de edad. Amsterdam se convirtió rápidamente en su hogar.

El nuevo apartamento de los Frank no era tan grande como el de Frankfurt, pero tenía espacio para huéspedes. Otto y Edith extrañaban a su familia y a sus viejos amigos. Por eso, se pusieron muy contentos cuando Oma vino a vivir con ellos. Deseaban que otros parientes también los visitaran. Muchas familias judías se mudaron de Alemania a Amsterdam. Muy pronto, los Frank ya tenían un círculo de amistades judías alemanas. En la escuela, la mitad de los niños de la clase de Ana eran judíos. Algunos habían llegado de Frankfurt, igual que ella.

Ana era una buena estudiante, pero odiaba las matemáticas. Era muy parlanchina, y, con frecuencia, sus maestros tenían que regañarla para que se quedara callada. En su tiempo libre, le gustaba jugar ping-pong. Creó un club de ping-pong llamado "La osa menor menos 2". Tenía cinco miembros. El nombre del club venía de la cantidad de estrellas en la constelación Osa Menor. Ana creía que en

la constelación había cinco estrellas. En realidad, son siete. Esto explica el "menos 2" en el nombre del club.

A Ana le gustaba leer. Leía libros de historia y de mitos griegos, y una serie muy popular sobre una niña llamada Joop, aventurera y activa, como Ana.

También le gustaba patinar en el hielo y andar en bicicleta con su amiga Hanne. Hanne secundaba a Ana en todas sus travesuras.

A veces, se paraban en el balcón del departamento de los Frank y le echaban agua a la gente que pasaba por la calle.

Ana era buena nadadora. Amsterdam no estaba lejos de la costa. Ana y Margot aparecen en muchas fotos en la playa, en traje de baño. En una foto, la pequeña y delgada Ana sale arropada con una manta. Más tarde escribió que cuando tomaron la foto se estaba congelando del frío. A su madre solía preocuparle que pescara un catarro, pues Ana era muy enfermiza. Faltaba a la escuela con frecuencia porque tenía gripe y tos.

A Ana le encantaba ir al cine. Cortaba fotos de estrellas de cine de las revistas. Soñaba con llegar a ser una estrella de cine  algún día, pero no estaba segura de ser lo suficientemente bonita. Ana sentía que era como el patito feo.

En muchos aspectos, la infancia de Ana fue como la de la mayoría de los niños. Excepto que, de vez en cuando, sucedía algo temible.

En 1938, su tío Walter fue arrestado en Alemania por ser judío. Fue enviado a un campo de trabajo forzado. Era como una prisión. El tío Walter tuvo la suerte de recuperar la libertad gracias a que prometió dejar Alemania para siempre. Al final, se mudó a Estados Unidos.

LA ROSA BLANCA

No todos los alemanes creían en Adolfo Hitler ni en sus repugnantes ideas. Algunos se enfrentaron a los nazis, poniendo en riesgo su propia vida. En la ciudad de Munich, un grupo de estudiantes universitarios escribió unos panfletos contra los nazis que se repartieron por todo el país. El panfleto advertía que Hitler estaba destruyendo la libertad de los alemanes y que había llegado la hora de levantarse para exigir la justicia y tolerancia.

Shophie Scholl

Los líderes de estos estudiantes eran unos hermanos llamados Hans y Sophie Scholl. Llamaron a su grupo "La rosa blanca". Muy pronto, los nazis acabaron con La rosa blanca y mataron a sus líderes.

Hans Scholl

Hoy, muchas escuelas, calles y monumentos alemanes llevan el nombre de estos valientes jóvenes que no tuvieron miedo de hablar claro.

En realidad, ¿qué tan segura era Holanda? En 1938, Hitler unió Austria a Alemania. Austria limita con Alemania por el norte. Los austriacos hablaban alemán, y muchos se sentían felices de pertenecer

a este poderoso imperio. Vitoreaban a los soldados de Hitler cuando pasaban marchando por las
calles de Viena.

Los holandeses, por el contrario, odiaban a
Hitler. La mayoría de la gente no soportaba la idea
de vivir bajo su dominio. Pero, ¿importaba, en realidad, lo que ellos pensaran? En marzo de 1939,
Hitler invadió Checoslovaquia. ¿Qué tal si decidía
que Holanda también fuera parte del imperio?

Otto y Edith tenían que tomar una decisión difícil. ¿Debían quedarse en Amsterdam o mudarse
nuevamente? Y, si decidían mudarse, ¿a dónde
irían? ¿A Inglaterra? ¿A Estados Unidos? ¿A algún
país de América del Sur? Era muy difícil obtener el
permiso para vivir en otros países. Además, Ana y
su hermana eran felices en Amsterdam. Y, aunque
Edith no estaba feliz, le agradaba tener cerca a sus
parientes que seguían en Alemania. En 1939, Otto
Frank cumplió 50 años. Se sentía demasiado viejo
para comenzar una nueva vida.

Al final, los Frank decidieron no desarraigar a su familia por segunda vez. Se quedarían en Amsterdam.

Capítulo 3
Otra guerra mundial

Luego de que Hitler invadiera Polonia, en septiembre de 1939, Inglaterra y Francia le declararon la guerra. Así comenzó la Segunda Guerra Mundial. Italia se alió con Alemania. Por el momento, Estados Unidos, que estaba a un océano de distancia, permaneció fuera del conflicto.

El pequeño país de Holanda se mantuvo neutral, lo que significa que no se pondría del lado de ninguno de los dos bandos. Los holandeses pensaban que eso mantendría al ejército de Hitler lejos de ellos.

Por la noche, mientras tomaban café con pastel, los Frank y otras familias judías que vivían en Amsterdam hablaban sobre la guerra. Su sueño

era que Hitler fuera derrotado. Así, todos podrían regresar a Alemania. Seguían las noticias en la radio, pero nunca hablaban delante de los niños acerca de sus miedos respecto al futuro.

Los Frank continuaron con su vida como si nada estuviera pasando. Viajaban en familia. Pasaron unas vacaciones de verano en un pueblo costero de Bélgica. En una primavera, recorrieron los canales de Holanda en una casa flotante.

Durante los primeros meses de 1940, hizo un frío glacial. A Ana no le importaba. Los canales estuvieron congelados durante más tiempo del acostumbrado. Ana y sus amigas patinaban durante horas. Ahora tenía 10 años y medio, y anhelaba tener unos patines de verdad para poder saltar y hacer otros malabares en el hielo. Todo lo que ella tenía eran los viejos patines de Margot. Consistían en unas cuchillas que se sujetaban a sus zapatos con una llave.

Sus padres no tenían tiempo para pensar en patines. Estaban muy preocupados por la posibilidad de un ataque a Holanda. Llegaron varias advertencias sobre una supuesta invasión de los alemanes. Sin embargo, una y otra vez, resultaron ser sólo falsas alarmas.

Al final de la primavera, el tiempo se puso cálido y soleado. De repente, lo que todos más temían se hizo realidad. El 10 de mayo de 1940 Alemania invadió Holanda. Hitler había estado esperando a que mejorara el tiempo para enviar sus aviones. La mañana del ataque, cayeron bombas del cielo. Amsterdam se estremeció como si se tratara de un terremoto.

Dos días después cayeron más bombas. Se incendió el aeropuerto, y también el puerto marítimo. Sin embargo, Amsterdam había tenido suerte. Otra ciudad, Rotterdam, había sido destruida. Miles de personas murieron.

La reina de Holanda logró escapar a Inglaterra. Allí permaneció hasta el final de la guerra. Se mantuvo en contacto con su gente a través de la radio.

Les pidió que mantuvieran la calma. Sin embargo, no había servicio telefónico, ni autobuses ni trenes. Comenzó a cundir el pánico. Por el miedo a quedarse

sin comida, la gente compró todo lo que pudo en las tiendas de comestibles. Muy pronto, los estantes quedaron vacíos. Durante todo el día sonaron alarmas que advertían de nuevas bombas. Los holandeses eran prisioneros en su propio país.

Algunos judíos que vivían en Holanda trataron de salir del país en ferry, pero muy pocos lo lograron.

Los Frank ni siquiera intentaron escapar. No tenían auto. Además, la abuela de Ana era vieja y estaba muy enferma. No podía viajar.

Los padres de Ana habían tenido que huir a Amsterdam para escapar de los alemanes. Ahora, los alemanes habían llegado a Amsterdam. No tenían a dónde huir. Su única alternativa era esconderse.

La Resistencia

Bandas de combatientes judíos hicieron lo que pudieron para detener a los nazis. Estos combatientes clandestinos eran llamados partisanos y solían actuar con el apoyo de personas que no eran judías.

El levantamiento más famoso se llevó a cabo en Varsovia, Polonia. Durante la Segunda Guerra Mundial, en muchas ciudades los judíos fueron obligados a vivir en vecindarios separados llamados *ghettos*. El ghetto más grande estaba en Varsovia.

En 1943, los judíos del ghetto de Varsovia se habían dado cuenta de que el ser enviados a un campo de concentración era una sentencia de muerte. También sabían que no tenían ninguna esperanza de vencer a los nazis. No tenían prácticamente armas y estaban atrapados en el ghetto. Aun así, decidieron luchar. Lograron sostener el levantamiento durante casi un mes. Unos 7,000 de los 60,000 judíos que vivían en el ghetto murieron en la rebelión. De los que quedaron, 50,000 fueron capturados y enviados a campos de concentración.

Hoy existen monumentos levantados en honor de los héroes del ghetto de Varsovia en varias ciudades de Europa y Estados Unidos.

Capítulo 4
¡Ocupados!

Holanda era ahora un país ocupado. Eso significa que los alemanes tenían el control. Se izaron banderas

nazis. Inmediatamente, la vida de todo el mundo comenzó a cambiar; pero más aún para los judíos.

Ahora, todos los judíos —incluidos los niños, como Ana y su hermana— tenían que registrarse con los alemanes. Nadie más tenía que hacerlo. Los alemanes querían seguirle la pista a todos los judíos. Querían saber quiénes eran y dónde vivían. Los judíos tuvieron que entregar casi todo su dinero a los nazis. Sus negocios fueron cerrados. (Otto le entregó su empresa a dos buenos amigos que no eran judíos y que trabajaban con él). Los judíos que trabajaban en empresas cuyos dueños no eran judíos perdieron su trabajo.

Se prohibieron los libros y las películas hechos por judíos. Ni siquiera se les permitía ir al cine. Eso debió haber molestado mucho a Ana. Sus padres hicieron todo lo que pudieron. Alquilaban películas y proyectores para verlas en casa. Ana y su amiga Jackie hacían boletos y conducían a la gente hasta su asiento. La madre de Ana servía meriendas.

Había ataques sorpresivos contra los judíos. Un sábado por la tarde, un grupo encabezado por soldados alemanes golpeó y arrestó a 400 hombres judíos. Otto Frank tuvo la suerte de no haber sido alcanzado por la redada. Los hombres arrestados fueron enviados a campos de concentración. Sólo uno de ellos regresó a la ciudad.

Los holandeses estaban furiosos. Organizaron una huelga. Una mañana de febrero, a las 10:30 a.m., todo el mundo paró de trabajar en toda Holanda.

Se interrumpió el servicio de tranvías. Se cerraron todas las tiendas. Los restaurantes no sirvieron comida.Se cerraron las fábricas. El país entero participó en

la huelga. Para los holandeses, era la manera de decirle a Hitler lo que pensaban de él: que el trato que les daba a los judíos era equivocado, injusto e inhumano.

¿Sirvió esto para detener a los alemanes? No. En
este punto, los padres de Ana ya no podían ocul-
tarle a sus hijas lo que estaba sucediendo. Había
avisos en las bancas de los parques que decían
"Prohibido para los judíos". A los judíos de Holanda
ya no se les permitía entrar a bibliotecas, museos, sa-
las de concierto, restaurantes, ni siquiera, al zoológico.

En ese verano, se les prohibió a los judíos usar las playas y piscinas públicas. No podían visitar ni los parques públicos ni los hoteles. Todo esto era horrible para todos, pero especialmente para los niños, como Ana. Había llegado el verano, pero no tenían dónde ir a divertirse.

Cada vez que perdían algo más, los judíos tenían la esperanza de que no iba a suceder nada peor. De hecho, los Frank todavía disfrutaban momentos felices. Ana pasaba parte de sus vacaciones en el campo, con la familia de su amiga Sanne. Fue allí donde comenzó a sentir interés por los chicos.

También hubo una boda. Los Frank eran muy cercanos a una joven mujer holandesa que se llamaba Miep y trabajaba en la fábrica de pectina. Ni ella ni su esposo, Jan Gies, eran judíos, pero Miep conocía a Otto desde hacía muchos años y lo respetaba mucho. Era especialmente cercana a Ana. La niña no lo sabía en aquel momento, pero la pareja iba a desempeñar un importante papel en su vida.

Capítulo 5
Las estrellas amarillas

Los nazis les arrebataron a los judíos sus derechos, uno por uno. A los alemanes además les daba placer hacer espectáculos públicos con los judíos. Querían avergonzarlos. En el verano de 1941, los nazis decidieron que los niños judíos no podían regresar a sus antiguas escuelas. Ahora tendrían que asistir a escuelas separadas, sólo para judíos.

Sin embargo, no hicieron el anuncio durante el verano, sino que esperaron a que comenzaran las clases. Entonces, sacaron a los niños judíos de sus salones de clase. Era una manera de hacer que esos niños, como Ana, se sintieran marginados. Por lo menos, en su nueva escuela, Ana quedó en la misma clase que su amiga Hanne. Además, algunas cosas no cambiaron. Los maestros todavía regañaban a Ana por hablar todo el tiempo.

En abril de 1942, los nazis obligaron a todos los judíos mayores de seis años de edad a llevar un gran parche en la ropa. Era una estrella judía de color amarillo. La estrella judía, también llamada estrella de David, es una estrella de seis puntas formada por dos triángulos. Es el símbolo más famoso de la religión judía. Tenían que llevarlo en el abrigo y en la chaqueta o el vestido. Había que coserlo en el pecho, donde todo el mundo lo pudiera ver.

LA ESTRELLA DE DAVID

Según cuenta la leyenda, la estrella de David estaba dibujada en el escudo del rey David, un antiguo rey de Israel que era sabio y heroico.

Hitler decidió que todos los judíos debían llevar una estrella de tela amarilla del tamaño de la mano de un adulto. Lo hizo para marcarlos. En el centro del parche estaba la palabra *jood*, que significa judío, escrito en letras que parecían hebreo.

A pesar de que se suponía que era un distintivo vergonzoso, muchos judíos llevaban su parche con orgullo.

En 1948, al poco tiempo de finalizar la Segunda Guerra Mundial, nació el nuevo estado de Israel. Se creó para que fuera la patria de todos los judíos. La estrella de David aparece en la bandera de Israel.

Desde hacía un tiempo, a los judíos no se les permitía tener auto. Ahora, se les comenzó a prohibir andar en bicicleta. Se dictó un toque de queda según el cual todos los judíos debían estar en su casa a las 8 en punto de la noche. No podían volver a salir hasta las 6 en punto de la mañana siguiente. Salir al propio balcón o sentarse en el jardín de la propia casa era considerado "estar afuera". Cualquier judío que estuviera

donde se suponía que no debía estar era arrestado, inclusive los niños.

La única buena noticia era que las fuerzas de Hitler habían comenzado a perder terreno en la guerra. Los alemanes habían invadido Francia, pero no eran capaces de invadir Inglaterra. Entonces, en diciembre de 1941, Estados Unidos entró en la guerra. Los Frank esperaban que aquello significara la derrota de Hitler. Pronto terminaría la pesadilla, y la vida volvería a la normalidad.

Capítulo 6
Kitty

El día que Ana cumplió trece años, en junio de 1942, alguien muy importante estuvo ausente. Oma había muerto aquel invierno. Ana dijo que sin su abuela ese cumpleaños no significaba mucho. Sin embargo, en la casa de los Frank siempre había lindas fiestas de cumpleaños. Ese año, Ana invitó tanto a

chicos como a chicas. Su madre horneó un fabuloso pastel, y su padre puso una película sobre un valiente perro llamado Rin Tin Tin.

Ésta fue la última fiesta de cumpleaños de verdad que tuvieron los Frank. Ana recibió muchos regalos de su familia: libros, un rompe-cabezas, un prendedor, caramelos. Pero hubo un regalo que ella apreció más que los demás: un pequeño cuaderno forrado con una tela a cuadros de color rojo y verde, con un cerrojo. En la parte interior de la cubierta, Ana puso una foto suya. Al lado escribió: "¡Qué guapa! ¿Verdad?"

Ana le dio a su diario el nombre de "Kitty" en honor a una vieja amiga que se llamaba así. Dos días después de su cumpleaños, Ana escribió por primera vez en su diario. Siempre comenzaba con "Querida

Kitty". Ana le contó a Kitty todo. Le habló de un chico que le gustaba llamado Hello, de las peleas que tenía con sus amigas, de los libros que había disfrutado. Todo. Kitty era una amiga con la que nunca discutía y que siempre escuchaba.

Menos de un mes más tarde, Ana tuvo que darle a Kitty una horrible noticia. Un domingo por la tarde, a comienzos de julio de 1942, llegó por correo una notificación. ¡Margot iba a ser enviada a un campo de trabajo forzado en Alemania! Se le ordenaba llegar a la estación de trenes con sus pertenencias y suficiente comida para un viaje de tres días.

Los nazis habían comenzado a formar grupos de judíos para los campos de trabajo forzado. Se llevaban cientos todos los días. Edith había pensado que quizás arrestarían a su esposo, pero jamás pensó que se llevarían a su hija. Margot tenía tan sólo 16 años. Los alemanes habían prometido no separar a las familias.

A pesar de todo, Otto y Edith no iban a permitir que se llevaran a su hija. La única salida era hacer lo que otros judíos estaban haciendo. La familia completa tenía que desaparecer lo antes posible. Como muy tarde, a la mañana siguiente.

Lo que Ana y su hermana no sabían era que su padre ya había encontrado un escondite. Estaba junto al edificio donde quedaban las oficinas de su compañía. Había unas escaleras secretas que conducían a un grupo de habitaciones.

La parte de atrás del anexo secreto

Otto y Edith llevaban varios meses preparando el escondite. Todas las noches llevaban muebles, platos, cubiertos, ropa de cama. Tuvieron cuidado de llevar las cosas poco a poco. Se construyó un baño con inodoro. También había una estufa. Lo que los Frank estaban haciendo no era algo extraño. En 1942 y 1943, entre 20 y 30 mil judíos que vivían en Holanda se escondieron.

Aquella noche, Margot y Ana metieron algunas cosas personales en el bolso escolar. Ana empacó rulos, pañuelos, libros, un peine y algunas cartas. Las niñas no sabían adónde iban. Ana no pudo despedirse de ninguna de sus amigas. Otto dejó en el apartamento una nota con una dirección en Suiza para que pensaran que habían salido de Holanda.

A la mañana siguiente, las niñas se pusieron varias capas de ropa bajo la gabardina. Llevar maletas era muy arriesgado. Los Frank cerraron la puerta de la casa en la que habían vivido durante ocho años. Ana apenas tuvo tiempo de abrazar a su amado gatito negro. Estaba segura de que regresaría a casa pronto. Sabía que los vecinos cuidarían al pequeño Moortje. Aun así, sus ojos estaban llenos de lágrimas.

Ana se aseguró de llevar una cosa en su equipaje: su diario forrado con una tela a cuadros. Iba en su bolso escolar.

Esto es lo que Ana llevaba puesto: dos suéteres, tres pares de pantalones; encima, un vestido, una falda, una chaqueta, una pantaloneta de verano, dos pares de medias, zapatos de amarrar, una gorra y una bufanda.

Capítulo 7
El anexo secreto

¿Cómo era la vida en el escondite, o el "anexo secreto", como lo llamaban?

Primero que todo, el escondite era bastante pequeño. A pesar de que tenía dos plantas, el espacio total era de tan sólo 50 yardas cuadradas. Detrás de la puerta secreta había dos habitaciones: una con una estufa y un fregadero, y el baño. En el piso de arriba había otros dos cuartos muy pequeños: uno para Edith y Otto, y otro para Margot y Ana.

Afortunadamente para Ana, sus postales y fotos de estrellas de cine la estaban esperando.

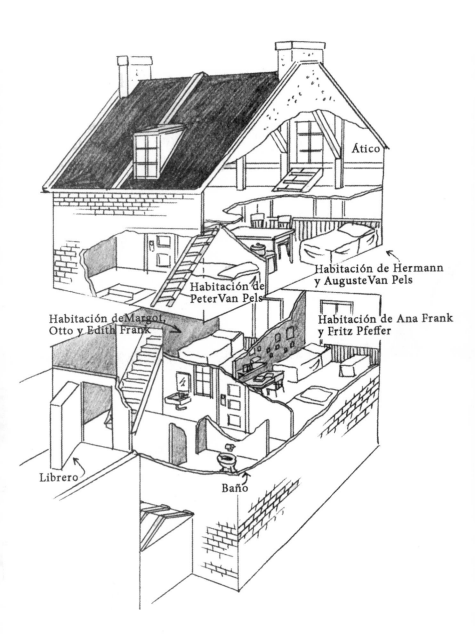

Ático

Habitación de Hermann y Auguste Van Pels

Habitación de Peter Van Pels

Habitación de Ana Frank y Fritz Pfeffer

Habitación de Margot, Otto y Edith Frank

Librero

Baño

UNA AFICIONADA AL CINE

Ana tenía una colección grande de postales y fotos de estrellas de cine. Le encantaban las películas, y una de sus estrellas favoritas era una actriz de Hollywood llamada Deanna Durbin, famosa por sus papeles en películas sobre adolescentes. A Ana también le fascinaban las familias reales. En la pared de su habitación en el anexo secreto tenía una postal con la imagen de las princesas Elizabeth y Margarita de Inglaterra. La princesa Elizabeth es hoy en día la reina Elizabeth II de Inglaterra.

Deanna Durbin

Ana dedicaba mucho tiempo a su colección de fotos y siempre estaba cambiando los recortes de revista y las postales, para hacer que su exhibición se mantuviera interesante. Las últimas fotos que puso en aquella pared todavía están allí.

La princesa Elizabeth
y la princesa Margarita

Su padre había traído las postales unos días antes. Ana pegó todas las que pudo en las vacías paredes de su habitación para alegrarla un poco.

Los alimentos se almacenaban en el ático, que tenía dos ventanas pequeñas. Desde una de las ventanas, Ana podía ver una alta torre con un reloj. Desde la otra, se veía un enorme castaño. Ana subía con frecuencia al ático, para estar a solas y pensar.

Una de las primeras cosas que hicieron Ana y su padre fue cubrir las ventanas con unas viejas cortinas. No podían arriesgarse a que alguien los viera desde fuera. Durante el día, todos tenían que caminar descalzos y susurrar. No podían usar el baño ni abrir un grifo entre las 9 de la mañana y las 7 de la noche. Alguien en el edificio de oficinas adjunto podría oírlos. Según Ana, todos vivían "tan callados como un bebé de ratón". La basura se quemaba en la estufa. Había que hacerlo cuando oscurecía, para evitar que el humo que salía de la chimenea fuera a llamar la atención de alguien.

Era un lugar muy estrecho en el que sólo estaban los Frank. Una semana más tarde llegó otra familia a vivir allí. Eran amigos de los Frank: el señor y la señora Van Pels, y su único hijo, Peter, que tenía 15 años. Peter llegó con su gato, Mouschi.

Cinco meses después, otra persona se unió al grupo: un hombre llamado Fritz Pfeffer. A Ana le pareció que era una persona remilgada y aburrida.

La familia Van Pels

Sin embargo, terminó teniendo que compartir su habitación con él, y Margot se pasó a la de sus padres.

La conexión principal de los Frank con el mundo exterior era Miep. Hubo otras tres personas ayudándolos: otra mujer joven de la compañía de pectina llamada Bep y los dos hombres que ahora estaban a cargo del negocio de Otto.

Fritz Pfeffer

Se llamaban Victor y Johannes. Estas personas estaban arriesgando su propia vida. Sin embargo, estaban dispuestos a hacer lo que fuera posible por sus amigos.

Miep solía llegar a primera hora de la mañana cuando todavía no había nadie en las oficinas. La madre de Ana o la señora Van Pels le daban la lista de compras.

Bep Voskuijl

Miep Gies

A la hora del almuerzo, ella o uno de los otros "colaboradores" regresaba con los comestibles. Miep también les llevaba libros, periódicos y noticias de lo que estaba pasando afuera. Ana siempre estaba ansiosa de saber cómo estaban sus amigas.

A pesar de que las ocho personas permanecían todo el tiempo juntas en el escondite, Ana se sentía sola en el anexo. Ella y su hermana nunca habían sido

muy cercanas. Margot era la favorita de mamá. Era bonita, inteligente y perfecta. A su lado, Ana siempre se sentía en el segundo puesto para todo. No obstante, Ana terminó haciéndose buena amiga de Peter Van Pels. A Ana le hacía muy feliz el tener la compañía de Peter. Con el tiempo, comenzó a gustarle, y le contó a Kitty que él le había dado su primer beso. Ana escribió: "Ya no estoy sola; él me ama. Yo lo amo".

Durante el día, Ana, Margot y Peter dedicaban bastante tiempo a leer sus textos escolares. Otto Frank los ayudaba a estudiar. Tenían clases de historia, literatura,

Peter Van Pels

idiomas extranjeros, geografía y matemáticas. Ana seguía odiando las matemáticas, pero deseaba mantenerse al día con las clases. Lo mismo pasaba con Margot y Peter. Los tres esperaban volver muy pronto a la escuela. Más adelante, aprendieron taquigrafía, que es un método para escribir rápido.

Con tanta gente viviendo en un espacio tan pequeño, era normal que hubiera peleas. A Ana le sorprendía ver que los adultos discutieran tanto. Con frecuencia, las discusiones eran por Ana, por

supuesto. Los padres de Peter pensaban que Ana era una malcriada. El señor Pfeffer también. Edith Frank discutía con su hija menor mucho más que antes. Sin embargo, aunque los ánimos estuvieran encendidos, nadie podía gritar ni hacer una escena. Era demasiado peligroso.

A veces, por la noche, bajaban a las oficinas. No era como salir a la calle, pero al menos Ana podía ver a la gente pasar desde la ventana.

Era precisamente por las noches, sin embargo, cuando Ana se sentía más triste. Pensaba en todas las cosas que había perdido: sus amigos, su gato, la sensación de recibir el sol sobre la piel, el olor del césped y de las flores. Ana se desahogaba en su diario. También escribía sobre lo que pasaba en el anexo, historias que recordaba de su infancia e incluso cuentos de hadas que ella misma se inventaba.

Los días se convirtieron en semanas, y las semanas en meses. Llegó el invierno. Ana llevaba seis meses viviendo en el anexo secreto. Ahora, a las 4:30 de la tarde, ya estaba oscuro afuera. No podían prender las luces. Eso podría atraer la atención de alguien. Como pasatiempo, jugaban a las adivinanzas y hablaban sobre libros que habían leído. Incluso, trataron de hacer ejercicio en la oscuridad.

El aburrimiento era espantoso. Sin embargo, no era tan malo como el miedo a ser descubiertos. Un día, alguien llamó a la puerta del anexo secreto. ¿Eran soldados nazis? ¿Vendrían a arrestarlos a todos? ¡No! Afortunadamente, era uno de sus colaboradores. Les avisó que un carpintero estaba trabajando en una oficina cercana; que no se preocuparan si escuchaban algún ruido. En otra ocasión, Peter dejó caer un enorme bulto de frijoles de 50 libras. El saco se rompió y montones de frijoles se desparramaron bulliciosamente por todas partes. A Ana le pareció divertido. Los frijoles le llegaban a los tobillos. Sin embargo, era muy arriesgado hacer cualquier ruido.

Por la noche, podían escuchar el sonido estruen-

doso de los aviones. Ana sabía que eran aviones de los
Aliados, que iban a bombardear ciudades alemanas.
La guerra se había volteado en contra de Hitler. Ana
esperaba que Alemania se rindiera, y pronto. Aun así,
el ruido de los aviones la asustaba. Corría a buscar
consuelo con su padre. Él era el único de la familia
que nunca la regañaba y que siempre estaba dispuesto
a consolarla.

En la primavera de 1943 comenzó a escasear la
comida en Holanda. Cada vez era más difícil para

Miep y los otros colaboradores llevar provisiones al anexo secreto.

Ya había pasado un año. Se acabaron todas las páginas del diario de Ana, pero Miep le llevó papel para que pudiera seguir escribiéndole a Kitty. Los temas sobre los que Ana escribía ya no eran los mismos. Se había vuelto más seria. Con frecuencia, pensaba en la guerra. "¿Para qué, para qué sirve la guerra? ¿Por qué la gente no puede convivir en paz?", le preguntó a Kitty.

Ana estaba cambiando. Se estaba convirtiendo en una jovencita. En una pared de la habitación de sus padres, iban marcando la altura de la niñas. ¡Ana había crecido más de cinco pulgadas! La ropa le quedaba pequeña. Su mente también había madurado. Ya no era una niña ruidosa.

Miep y Jan

Ana deseaba, más que cualquier otra cosa, que Miep y su esposo pasaran una noche en el anexo. Ellos la complacieron el día de su primer aniversario de bodas.

Muchos años después, Miep escribió un libro sobre los Frank en el cual habló de aquella noche. Ana quería que esa noche fuera como una gran fiesta. Diseñó un menú especial. Les puso a los platos nombres elegantes. Miep dice que Ana los atendió como si fueran estrellas de cine.

Esa noche se quedaron en la habitación de Ana. El anexo secreto era tan pequeño que Miep podía oír hasta el más leve de los sonidos —como el de una pantufla al caer al suelo o el de alguien tosiendo en su cama. Miep iba al anexo casi todos los días para ver a sus amigos. Jan también había estado allí muchas veces. Sin embargo, estar allí, acostados en la oscuridad, era algo diferente. Miep sentía miedo. Se sobresaltaba con cualquier ruido pequeño. ¿Acaso estaba alguien entrando al anexo secreto? De repente, Miep comprendió lo que era esconderse. ¡Era terrorífico! Y eso que Miep y Jan sólo lo hicieron durante una noche.

Otra cosa buena era que Ana ya no se peleaba tanto con su hermana. Se estaban haciendo amigas. Ana también estaba comenzando a comprender mejor a su madre.

Una noche, Ana estaba escuchando la radio. Era una transmisión en holandés desde Londres.

Un hombre dijo que al terminar la guerra se publicarían diarios y cartas. Ana comenzó a soñar con ver su diario algún día convertido en un libro. Un libro que otros leerían. Le escribió a Kitty: "Desde hace rato sabes que mi gran deseo es convertirme algún día en periodista y más tarde en una escritora famosa… Después de la guerra, quiero publicar un libro que se llamará *El anexo secreto*. No sé si lo lograré".

Capítulo 8
¡Atrapados!

Cuando Ana cumplió 15 años, las familias llevaban ya casi dos años escondidos: más de 650 días. Era el mes de junio de 1944. La guerra estaba llegando a su fin. Italia, que antes era aliado de Alemania, se había rendido.

Las fuerzas Aliadas estaban liberando Francia. En un mapa que tenía pegado a una pared del anexo, Otto iba marcando el avance de los Aliados. Para Ana, era como si los amigos se estuvieran acercando. Comenzó a ver la libertad en el futuro cercano.

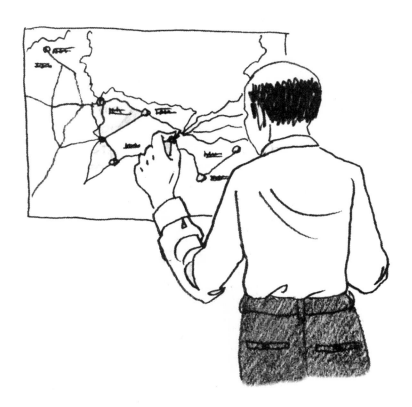

El 15 de julio de 1944, escribió: "Creo que todo va a arreglarse; que esta crueldad va a terminar... Mientras tanto, debo mantener vivos mis ideales, ¡pues es probable que llegue el momento en que pueda hacerlos realidad!".

Dos líderes

Durante al Segunda Guerra Mundial, el primer ministro de Gran Bretaña, Winston Churchill, y el presidente de Estados Unidos, Franklin D. Roosevelt, no sólo permanecieron unidos en contra de los alemanes sino que además se convirtieron en amigos personales muy cercanos. Roosevelt estaba en su tercer período como presidente cuando Estados

Winston Churchill

Unidos se unió a las fuerzas aliadas, a fines de 1941. Este hecho fue decisivo para darle un vuelco al curso de la guerra. Roosevelt y Churchill se reunían en secreto para coordinar los ataques contra su enemigo común. Franklin Roosevelt, que había padecido polio y usaba silla de ruedas, es considerado uno de los mejores presidentes del país. Lamentablemente, Roosevelt murió en abril de 1945, apenas unos meses antes de que terminara la guerra.

Franklin D. Roosevelt

En la mañana del 4 de agosto de 1944, Peter escuchó unos gritos que venían de abajo. Eran voces de hombres. Con las armas en alto, un grupo de policías nazis asaltaron el anexo.

Después de tanto tiempo, después de haber sido tan cuidadosos, los habían atrapado. Todo había terminado.

Alguien los traicionó; pero, ¿quién pudo haber sido? Nunca se supo. Con seguridad, no fue ninguno de los colaboradores.

Después de que se llevaron a Ana y a los demás, Miep se coló en el anexo. Quería entrar antes de que los nazis regresaran a desocuparlo. Miep encontró el diario de Ana en el piso. Había hojas dispersas por todas partes. Miep recogió todo, y también el álbum de fotos de los Frank, y lo puso en un cajón bajo llave. Esperaba poder devolverle todo a la familia después de la guerra.

Las ocho personas que estaban en el anexo fueron a parar a un campo de concentración en Polonia. A Peter, Otto y los señores Pfeffer y Van Pels los llevaron con los hombres.

A Ana, Margo, Edith y la señora Van Pels las pusieron con las mujeres.

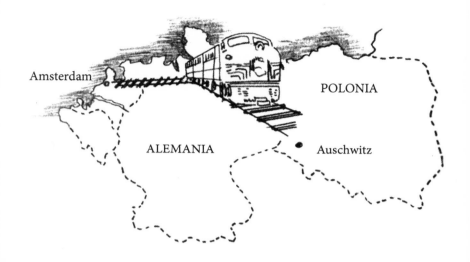

Amsterdam

POLONIA

ALEMANIA

Auschwitz

En el campo de concentración, a la mayoría de las personas las mataban de inmediato. Sin embargo, para aquellos que quedaban vivos, la vida no podía llamarse vida en absoluto. Los sobrevivientes dicen que es imposible describir lo horrible que era aquello. Margot y Ana estaban ahora separadas de sus padres. Las dos lucharon por sobrevivir, pero se enfermaron de tifus. Murieron en marzo de 1945.

En abril, soldados británicos tomaron el campo de concentración y liberaron a todos los que quedaban vivos. Había terminado la guerra. Por fin. Sin embargo, ya era demasiado tarde para Ana Frank.

Capítulo 9
Un sueño se hace realidad

De las ocho personas que vivieron en el anexo, sólo Otto Frank sobrevivió a la guerra. Regresó a Amsterdam con la esperanza de reencontrarse con su familia. Por el contrario, lo único que encontró fue la noticia de que su esposa y sus hijas habían muerto. Todo lo que le quedó de ellas fue el diario y las fotografías que Miep había guardado.

Otto sabía que Ana estaba llevando un diario, pero no tenía ni idea de cuánto había escrito. Tampoco sabía lo bellas que eran sus palabras.

Otto transcribió varias páginas en máquina de escribir para que su madre y sus amigos las leyeran. Todos lo instaron a que le mostrara el diario de Ana a las editoriales. El mundo tenía que saber de esta extraordinaria jovencita.

En el verano de 1947, el sueño de Ana se hizo realidad. Su diario se convirtió en un libro. Ana era una autora publicada. Primero se llamó *El anexo*

secreto. Más tarde, el título cambió a *Ana Frank: el diario de una jovencita*. En español se llama *El diario de Ana Frank*.

Hitler había asesinado a seis millones de judíos. Eso es un hecho verídico —un hecho horrible— y aun así resulta difícil de comprender. Cuando uno lee acerca de la vida de una niña que murió a causa de Hitler, se hace más fácil entender lo sucedido. El diario de Ana puso un enorme y espantoso suceso en el plano personal. Lo que vemos es a una niña con esperanzas y sueños que todo lo que pedía era tener oportunidad de vivir su vida.

Durante los años que siguieron, el diario de Ana se volvió famoso en todo el mundo. Ha sido traducido a más de 65 idiomas. Otto Frank murió en 1980 a los 91 años de edad. Dedicó todos esos años a mantener viva la memoria de Ana y su familia.

Otto hizo un buen trabajo. En 1960, el anexo secreto se abrió al público. Cada año lo visitan cerca de un millón de personas. Ya no están los muebles,

pero las fotos de Ana de sus estrellas de cine favoritas aún están en la pared. Los visitantes pueden ver el lugar donde ocho personas lucharon para aferrarse a la vida de la única manera que podían hacerlo: escondiéndose.

Las últimas palabras de este libro sobre Ana son de ella misma. En su diario, Ana escribió: "A pesar de todo todavía creo que, en realidad, en el fondo de su corazón, la gente es buena".

LÍNEA CRONOLÓGICA DE LA VIDA DE ANA FRANK

1929 —— Nace Ana Frank el 12 de junio, en Frankfurt, Alemania.

1933 —— Edith y Margot Frank se mudan a Holanda.

1934 —— Ana y su padre se reúnen con el resto de la familia en Amsterdam.

1941 —— Ana y Margot asisten a la Escuela Judía de Amsterdam.

1942 —— El 12 de junio Ana cumple 13 años y recibe un diario como regalo de cumpleaños; el 6 de julio la familia Frank se esconde en el anexo secreto.

1944 —— En agosto, los residentes del anexo secreto son arrestados y enviados a campos de concentración.

1945 —— Muere Edith Frank, el 26 de enero; Ana y Margot mueren de tifus, en marzo; Otto Frank regresa a Amsterdam el 3 de junio.

1947 —— Se publican 1,500 ejemplares del diario de Ana en Amsterdam.

1952 —— El diario de Ana se traduce al inglés.

1955 —— Se estrena en Broadway una obra de teatro basada en el diario de Ana Frank.

1960 —— Se abre al público el anexo secreto.

LÍNEA CRONOLÓGICA DEL MUNDO

Termina la Primera Guerra Mundial. — **1918**

El partido Nazi celebra su primera convención en Munich, Alemania. — **1923**

Se estrena *El cantante de jazz*, la primera película con diálogos sonoros; — **1927**
cae la Bolsa de Valores de Nueva York, originando la Gran Depresión.

Adolfo Hitler es nombrado canciller de Alemania; empresas judías — **1933**
son boicoteadas; se forma la gestapo (policía secreta).

Se celebran los Juegos Olímpicos en Berlín, Alemania; se estrena — **1936**
la película *Three Smart Girls*, protagonizada por Deanna Durbin.

Franklin D. Roosevelt inicia su segundo período — **1937**
como presidente de EE.UU.

Hitler invade Polonia; comienza la Segunda Guerra Mundial. — **1939**

Los japoneses bombardean Pearl Harbor; — **1941**
EE.UU. entra en la Segunda Guerra Mundial.

Ejecutan a Sophie Scholl, líder de la Rosa Blanca. — **1943**

Hitler se suicida en un búnker secreto; Alemania se rinde — **1945**
y termina la Segunda Guerra Mundial.

La princesa Elizabeth se convierte en Elizabeth II, reina de Inglaterra. — **1952**

Elvis Presley se presenta en el programa — **1956**
de televisión *The Ed Sullivan Show*.

John F. Kennedy es elegido presidente de EE.UU. — **1960**

¿Quién fue...?

¿Quién fue Albert Einstein?

¿Quién fue Amelia Earhart?

¿Quién fue Ana Frank?

¿Quién fue Benjamín Franklin?

¿Quién fue Fernando de Magallanes?

¿Quién fue Harriet Tubman?

¿Quién fue Harry Houdini?

¿Quién fue Mark Twain?

¿Quién fue el rey Tut?

¿Quién fue Tomás Jefferson?